BE
THE
BEST
AT
WHAT
MATTERS
MOST

BE
THE
BEST
AT
WHAT
MATTERS
MOST

The Only
Strategy You Will Ever Need

JOE

CALLOWAY

WILEY

Cover design: C. Wallace

Published by John Wiley & Sons, Inc., Hoboken, New Jersey.
Published simultaneously in Canada.

For general information about our other products and services, please contact our Customer Care Department within the United States at (800) 762-2974, outside the United States at (317) 572-3993 or fax (317) 572-4002.

Wiley publishes in a variety of print and electronic formats and by print-on-demand. Some material included with standard print versions of this book may not be included in e-books or in print-on-demand. If this book refers to media such as a CD or DVD that is not included in the version you purchased, you may download this material at http://booksupport.wiley.com. For more information about Wiley products, visit www.wiley.com.

Library of Congress Cataloging-in-Publication Data:

Calloway, Joe.

Be the best at what matters most : the only strategy you will ever need / Joe Calloway.

pages cm

Includes index.

ISBN 978-1-118-56987-0 (cloth); ISBN 978-1-118-61124-1 (ebk);
ISBN 978-1-118-61118-0 (ebk); ISBN 978-1-118-61119-7 (ebk)

1. Strategic planning. 2. Consumer satisfaction. 3. Success in business. I. Title.

HD30.28.C3475 2013
658.4'012—dc23

2012048023

Printed in the United States of America

10 9 8 7 6 5 4 3 2 1

Always for Annette, Jessica, and Cate.
Special thanks to my best friend and business partner,
Kris Young, and to my friends, Matthew Holt and
the wonderful team at John Wiley & Sons.

Contents

1

The Only Strategy You Will Ever Need

Building Business at Bill's Burgers

Bill owns a hamburger restaurant called Bill's Burgers. Bill needs more customers. So Bill does what any bright, energetic entrepreneur would do: He looks for ways to build his business.

Bill has read lots of articles about the power of the Internet. Bill has decided to make a video about Bill's Burgers, put it on YouTube, and have it go viral. In the video he plans to have babies doing funny things with hamburgers; some cute, playful puppies wearing tiny Bill's Burgers T-shirts; and hopefully Jennifer Aniston enjoying a Bill's Burger burger. The video will go viral, and people will flock to Bill's Burgers in droves.

Of course, everyone knows that social media is the key to business success today. Bill is designing a Facebook page for his restaurant, and he is starting a blog. He thinks he'll call it Bill's Burger Blog. He will write about hamburgers and onion rings and the great things that happen in his restaurant. The blog will be connected to his new Twitter account, where he plans to regularly post 140-character updates on hamburgers and hamburger-related stuff.

"Amaze" and "Delight"

Bill also bought some books about business. Most of them say that he should be doing things that will make his business unique and one of a kind. They say that he needs to be wildly imaginative and innovative and do things that will "amaze" and "delight" his customers. Bill goes to hamburger restaurant conventions, and the speakers there tell really great stories about hamburger restaurants that have done the coolest, most amazing things with customers. Bill wants to be amazing, too.

Bill read in one of the books that to be amazing, you have to have a wow factor. He has decided to start giving every customer a tiny chocolate candy hamburger when they leave. He thinks this will be his wow factor. Bill also plans to have a magician circulate through the restaurant, doing card tricks and cutting a rope in half, then putting it back together again. People love magicians, and Bill is pretty sure that this will "amaze" and "delight" them and make Bill's Burgers unique and one of a kind. No other restaurant in town has a staff magician.

Moruga Scorpion Peppers

Because he is willing to go the extra mile in differentiating his business, Bill is also going to add some wildly unique items to his menu to set him apart from his competition. He is considering adding a Vanilla Burger, a Cheese-to-the-Max Burger with 11 different kinds of cheese, a Cinnamon Apple Burger, a Volcano Burger with Trinidad Moruga Scorpion peppers, and a Really-Ham Burger, made with ham.

Bill is exhausted from pursuing all of these ideas and activities, but he's excited because he is sure that by harnessing the power of the Internet and social media, having a wow factor and a magician who delights customers, and offering flavored hamburgers that are innovative and unique, his business will boom and he'll have more customers in no time.

What If He Made a Better Hamburger?

Some of these ideas may well be worth pursuing. But if Bill asked me for advice, I'd suggest a different approach. It's a wildly contrarian idea that flies in the face of much of what you read and hear today about what it takes to succeed in business.

I think Bill should begin by finding out what matters most to his customers, focusing there, and being the best at that. Maybe it's really all about just making better hamburgers. I wonder if Bill's thought about that.

What Do You Think?

You may be thinking, "It's not an either/or proposition. Maybe Bill should make better hamburgers *and* have a magician." You could be right. If a lot of Bill's customers are families with small children, the magician might be just the ticket. I'm not trying to sell the idea that we shouldn't do social media or try to delight customers with a magician. As for social media, I'm all in on the social media strategy. I just hired a social media company to work with our business. I'm simply putting forth the idea that if we do the handful of things that matter most, whatever those things may be, and if we do them better than our competition, then we win. That may include social media, candy hamburgers, and magicians. I'm just saying think about it. Pick your lanes carefully.

There's no absolute right or wrong here. You need to find out what works for you in your own version of the Bill's Burgers story.

An Undeniable Premise

Be the best at what matters most, and you will succeed.

Part of me says that I should now just write "The End" and leave it at that. But the realist in me knows that such a radical, contrarian, and amazingly simple idea will be met with skepticism and thus needs some fleshing out.

It is an undeniable premise. When you are the best at what matters most, you succeed. You may be thinking, "But surely there must be more to it than that." No, that's it. The very simplicity of the idea is what makes it so powerful.

We Make It Too Complex

In the movie *The Big Lebowski,* Walter says to The Dude, "That's right, Dude, the beauty of this is its simplicity. Once the plan gets too complex, everything can go wrong."

Exactly.

Walter is right; most of us actually *do* make the plan too complex. We do it because, contrary to what most people might think, it's much easier to make things complex. It takes a lot of hard work to, as Steve Jobs once said, "get your thinking clean enough to make things simple." But it's worth all the hard work, because if you're able to make things simple, you can move mountains.

This book is about simplifying how you think about and go about your business. Focusing on what matters most helps you maximize your effectiveness. It helps you avoid the painful truth of the old saying "You did a great job. But you did the *wrong* job."

That's the Problem

Sometimes a client will say to me, "Joe, I'm doing everything I can think of to improve my business, but it's not working." That's the problem. The winners in business aren't the ones who do the most things. The winners are the ones who do the most important things.

What if you, your team, or your entire organization had absolute clarity about what was most important, and that's where the energy was focused? Imagine the force multiplier of that kind of shared sense of direction, purpose, and priorities. That's our goal: to absolutely maximize your efficiency and, especially, your effectiveness.

We're going to look at this idea of what matters most from a number of different perspectives, or through a variety of "lenses."

It Ends Up Being about the Customer

One vitally important idea in this book is that, ultimately, be they large or small, in manufacturing, hospitality, or health care, providing cutting-edge technology or the most basic of products or services, all businesses that are able to create and sustain success will incorporate what matters most to the customer into their core strategy. This is the one element that isn't optional. The needs of the customer must be satisfied. At some point, someone has to buy something. This is the common denominator of all businesses.

One thing that I often hear from my clients is "Our business is different. Our business isn't like any other business." Well, we all like to think we're special, but your business really is pretty much like every other business in the ways that count the most. Really, it is.

Business is business, and although each organization is unique in some of the particulars and details, in the end we all make things, do things, or sell things with at least one of our goals being that people will pay us for doing it. The same idea holds true for a nonprofit organization if you think of gaining support, be it in the form of contributions or otherwise, as how you get "paid" so that you can do the work that helps your constituents.

Of course, you may also have bigger-picture goals such as wanting to change the world for the better or improve people's lives with your work, and that's wonderful. But at some point somebody has to pay for something, or you don't have a business; you have a hobby.

We will very purposefully explore many approaches to what matters most, with the purpose of raising questions that you, and only you, can answer for your business. But at our center will be this unifying principle of being the best at what matters the most to the customer.

You're Spread Too Thin

> Pressure is something you feel when you don't know what the hell you're doing.
>
> —*Peyton Manning*

There are a lot of people feeling pressure these days. It's not necessarily that, as Peyton Manning says, "you don't know what the hell you're doing." It's more likely that you're not focused on what you *should* be doing.

What keeps many people awake at night is that they know that their business should be doing a lot better than it is or that their own individual performance should be creating greater results than it is. Leaders may know that they have great people and a great product or service, but they're not producing the results that they should be producing with the resources they have.

Assuming you have the right people on board and you're good at the basics of your business, you probably have the same problem that many highly competitive individuals and organizations have: You're spread too thin. You're trying to do too much. You're using a flamethrower when you should be using a blue-tip flame from an acetylene torch. You need to focus. You need to pick a lane.

The Three or Four Things

It's frustrating, stressful, and exhausting to try to do the 1,000 things you think you have to do to succeed. It's also counter-productive. There are probably no more than three or four things you need to focus on as long as you do them exceptionally well.

If I just lost you with the idea of only needing to focus on three or four things, let me say it again with as much clarity as possible: If you do an extraordinary job on the three or four things that matter the most, not only will you succeed, you will likely succeed far beyond your expectations.

The reason people get sucked into the tornado of trying to do a thousand things each day is that they aren't focused on those core activities that can actually advance their strategies. Because you're not focused, you aren't winning on the basics, and that's when people start looking for gimmicks, shortcuts, or "silver bullets" to try to improve their results.

The cold, hard truth is that there are no shortcuts. There are no silver bullets. There are no gimmicks that can replace the reality of the marketplace—that, ultimately, quality wins.

You Don't Need Gimmicks

Let's get clear on what creates business success today. I recently heard someone say what so many people foolishly believe: "It's not enough to be the best anymore. You have to have a wow factor to set yourself apart."

Let me point out the screamingly obvious. If the market-place decides that you are the best, that's the biggest wow factor there is. Only those who are far from being the best would ever say that it's not enough.

If you truly are the best, you don't need gimmicks. But if your core value proposition is lacking, you'd better pile on all the glitz, buzzers, bells, and gimmicks you can and hope it will work. (It won't.) Let me say that again. If you are not able to compete on the basics, then you quite naturally look for gimmicks as wow factors instead of letting quality and consistency be your wow factors.

If you truly are the best at what you do, are competitively priced (which may mean that you are the highest priced, as long as the value justifies it), and you are easy to do business with, you win. Every shred of evidence in the marketplace is telling us that now, more than ever, quality performance is the one sure factor that drives success.

Don't confuse temporarily fashionable trends with sustained success. Don't confuse a catchy story with performance. Look at who leads markets over a period of years and is able to sustain that lead through changing markets and economic conditions; then study how they do it. They don't do it with contrived wow factors. They do it by dominating with quality and value. They do it with constant, relentless improvement and innovation. They do it by winning at the basics. That's how they wow, as in, "Wow, these guys are so good, and they're good every single time."

If You Win on the Basics, You Win It All

You goal should be to be so good at the basics that you are cutting edge. You'll see me refer to that idea again. It's become one of my mantras.

By the way, I know that I lose some people simply by using the word *basics*. There are those who will roll their eyes and say, "Being good at the basics isn't enough. That's just table stakes. That just gets you in the game."

Note that I'm not talking about just being good. I'm talking about being *so* good at the basics that you are extraordinary. I'm talking about not just being competitive but actually *winning* on the basics. Here's reality: If you win on the basics, you win it all.

There Are No Silver Bullets; There's Just the Bomb

I was in Orlando to give a speech on improving team performance to 500 entrepreneurs when a member of the audience came up to me and said, "I hope you've got some silver bullets for us today." Sorry. I've been studying how companies succeed for more than 30 years, and I've never seen a single silver bullet. Never seen a shortcut.

There aren't any silver bullets. Not one. There's quality. That's not a bullet. It's the bomb. It always wins.

Questions to Consider

Thinking about the Bill's Hamburgers story, consider these questions with your team:

- What's your equivalent of hamburgers? What's your core value offering?
- What's the main thing that draws customers to you?
- What if you were 20 percent better at that main thing?
- What if you had a different main thing?
- What if Bill made hamburgers so amazingly good that people practically knocked down his door to buy them?

- What's your version of that?
- If I ask you, your partners, or your employees what are the three things that matter most in your business, what would they say?
- What would your customers say is most important to them?
- Would your customers' thoughts on what matters most match with yours?
- More important than what anyone says, what do the people on your team do all day long every day?
- What do you do all day long every day?
- Are you doing the most important things?
- What is the one thing you are doing that you know is a waste of time?
- What kept you from creating greater value for your customers today?
- What activities by you and your team will create the greatest return on effort and investment?

Think about whether you agree or disagree with these ideas. If you have business partners or colleagues, discuss how these ideas might relate to you; what, if any, value they have for you and what new ideas they serve to bring up for you:

- Our business is very complicated. Agree or disagree?
- Our business is actually pretty simple. Agree or disagree?
- We could do better at doing the most important things. Agree or disagree?
- If we were more focused, we would be more effective. Agree or disagree?
- There are no shortcuts. There are no silver bullets. Agree or disagree?

2

It's Really Not That Complicated

Build Better Cars. Imagine That

In August 2012 the American Customer Satisfaction Index (ACSI) declared that customer satisfaction with major automakers had reached its highest level in almost 20 years. After years of dissatisfaction with the car companies, what had turned things around so dramatically?

David VanAmburg, managing director of ACSI, revealed the shocking and amazing reason for the improvement in customer satisfaction. "The automakers are paying more attention to improving the quality of the vehicles themselves," VanAmburg said. "This might be a little more real, a little more sustainable."

Wow. Imagine that. Customers become more satisfied when the manufacturers make better cars.

Let that sink in. In this age of businesses searching like mad for ways to win customers by being unique, unequalled, singular, unusual, awesome, astonishing, surprising, stunning, startling, and amazing, the car companies did something truly inside the box.

They made better cars. And it worked.

It's not necessarily easy, but it's not complicated.

Questions to Consider

- How can we improve the quality of our core product or service?
- What are three specific action steps that we can take beginning tomorrow morning to make that happen?
- Who is accountable for making that happen?

3

So Good at the Basics That You're Cutting Edge

Substance, Not Flash

When I say *cutting edge,* I mean being at the very front edge of creating value through innovation. I don't mean trendy or "all the rage," unless that rage is able to produce and sustain a profit. By *cutting edge,* I mean a company that people talk about and study because it is able to win customers and keep them. I'm talking about substance, not flash. Let me tell you where I got the idea of being so good at the basics that you're cutting edge.

A Powerful Lesson

One of the most talked-about companies in the past few years, along with companies such as Apple, Google, and Starbucks, has been Zappos.com. Zappos started out selling shoes on the Internet, which in and of itself is a pretty gutsy thing to do. Their main product is something that you almost have to try on to know if you want it.

Today, Zappos sells a lot more than shoes. You can Google the company and find countless articles about it. Not only do people talk about Zappos, but business leaders go to Las Vegas, where the company is located, to study it for ideas they can take back home and use. It's a profitable company with a following of devoted customers and fans. I could write an entire book about Zappos, but the chief executive officer (CEO), Tony Hsieh, already has. It's called *Delivering Happiness: A Path to Profits, Passion, and Purpose,* and I highly recommend it.

So I won't go into detail about the remarkable approach that Zappos takes to deliver on what matters most both to its customers and its employees. But I do want to share the powerful lesson I've learned during my interactive keynotes for business audiences around the country.

"I Love Them!"

I often ask my audience how many of them are customers of Zappos. Almost always, 5 to 10 percent of them raise their hands. I then ask "How do you like Zappos?" The most common answer is "I love them!" Other answers are still in the "love" category, including "They're fantastic!," "Wonderful!," and "They're great!" By the way, I am very purposefully adding those exclamation points because Zappos customers are almost always very enthusiastic about the company.

What They Do Particularly Well

Then I ask, "What do you think Zappos does particularly well?" Here are the four responses I hear most often:

- **Selection**
  Customers say that Zappos has a wonderful selection of shoes and any of the other products that they shop for.
- **Delivery**
  I make the joke, for those in the audience who haven't done business with Zappos, that you hit Send on your computer to complete your order, and your doorbell rings. Suffice it to say, their delivery is very, very fast.
- **Customer service**
  The Zappos customer service call center employees are legendary. I could tell you story after story of how they do whatever it takes to make the customer happy.
- **Return policy**
  Zappos has a 365-day 100 percent satisfaction return policy. You have up to one year to return any product for any reason whatsoever. And Zappos pays for the shipping.

Inside the Box

Here's the lesson. Zappos is considered one of the coolest, most progressive, most forward-thinking and innovative companies in the world. They are a case study for excellence, especially in creating amazing customer experiences. So how does Zappos do it? What rocket science do they tap into to be so extraordinary? What's the outside-the-box thinking that makes them so effective?

Selection, delivery, customer service, and return policy. That's it. Zappos is one of my poster companies for being the best at what matters most. They bring innovative, outside-the-box thinking to inside-the-box issues. They have so mastered those basics that they are on the covers of business magazines around the world. They create incredibly loyal, raving fans by winning in the place where all business is won or lost: inside the box.

They are so good at the basics that they are cutting edge.

Questions to Consider

- Are you cutting edge?
- If so, how will you stay at that cutting edge?
- If not, what do you need to work on right now to start to get there?

4

Deciding What Matters Most

Defining the Problem

Albert Einstein said, "If I had one hour to save the world, I would spend 55 minutes defining the problem and only 5 minutes finding the solution." So let's define the problem, or, more accurately, the opportunity, which in our case is deciding what matters most. The obvious questions are "How do I know what matters most?" and "How do we figure it out?"

There are any number of ways to go about determining what is, or should be, most important in your business and your work. Let's think it through by looking at the question from a number of different perspectives. At the end you can take those elements that resonate with you, the ones that feel right, and make your own determinations. For those of you who want this to be totally a "thinking thing" and not be about how it feels, that's fine. You can drive the whole process with numbers. Do it with metrics. That's an option.

You can see from the examples of successful companies and people throughout this book that there are almost unlimited perspectives on this. To try to name one approach as the correct one is simply silly. Who's right? Tony Hsieh with his very human, very heartfelt philosophy at Zappos that focuses on team and family as being most important or former Harvard Business School professor Gary Loveman, chief executive officer (CEO) of Harrah's Entertainment, who is driven purely by the numbers? They're both right, because their respective approaches work well for each of them, their teams, and their companies.

It's important to know that there simply is no one template or formula to figure out what matters most to you in your business. Too many people don't get it that business is a highly personal endeavor. I know successful business leaders who pay little attention to the numbers, believing that if they get the "heart" aspects right, the numbers will take care of themselves.

Others would say that, on the contrary, business is strictly about the numbers. I would say that either way, you choose your own very personal approach to business.

Somebody's Got to Buy

Perhaps the simplest definition of business I've seen is that business is an organization or economic system where goods and services are exchanged for one another or for money. Every business requires enough customers to whom its output can be sold on a consistent basis in order to make a profit. In other words, somebody's got to buy whatever it is you're selling. To that end, regardless of whatever else might matter most to you, at the end of the day you have to incorporate what matters most to the customer as part of your thinking and strategy.

We'll talk plenty more about being focused on what matters most to the customer. But let's consider some other perspectives on what matters most, all of which are legitimate. It's about choosing a focus or purpose that resonates with you and your team.

Here are a few approaches to what matters most. Think about which of these are a good fit with you and your business.

Maximize Profit

Without profit, you don't have a business. The profit motive, especially when shared throughout a company, can be a powerful way to create not only organizational focus but buy-in into a company's goals and objectives (see Chapter 14 on bytes of knowledge). Of course, every business endeavor has to make a profit at some point, or it's not viable. For some, profit can be the focus that drives the machine. For others, profit can simply be the by-product if they are successful at doing what matters most to them.

That's the way Ron Shaich, founder and co-CEO of Panera Bread Company, looks at what matters most. "When I was a young person," Shaich said, "I used to be worried about the P&L [profit and loss statement], and then I realized that what drives the P&L is getting the right stuff done right—the key initiatives. That's where I began to focus most of my time."

Make a Positive Difference in the World

Blake Mycoskie created TOMS Shoes after a 2006 trip to Argentina, where he was struck by the number of children there who had no shoes to wear. His company matches every pair of shoes purchased with a pair of new shoes given to a child in need. For some, serving a larger cause that helps make life better for people is what matters most.

Over the course of my career helping companies succeed and grow, I have worked with many people in every kind of business imaginable whose primary motivation was to, in some way, make the world a better place. To them, the profit is necessary and welcome, but it's not the point. Profit is secondary in terms of their own motivation to make a positive difference in the lives of their customers or the community.

Be Number One

Jack Welch, the legendary CEO of GE, for many years had an absolute policy that GE would be only in markets in which it could be number one or number two. He eventually changed that policy, as it was determined that GE was missing opportunities in markets where they could start small and then grow.

There are countless corporate vision statements that contain words to the effect of "We will be number one in the supplying of . . ." or "We will be the recognized market leader in the servicing of . . . ." Part of what drives strategy and action in those companies is, quite simply, winning.

The purely competitive spirit is a powerful driver in many people. The potential danger of this strategy is that it can lead to a focus on the competition. You can't focus in two directions at once. If your attention is occupied by your competitor, then it's not on the customer. Your decisions can become driven by what your competitor is doing, rather than by how you can create value for the customer. This is a slippery slope and can make you vulnerable in a customer-driven marketplace.

Satisfy the Customer

For many, this is it. The idea is that if we take care of our customers, they will take care of us. There are any number of ways to think about satisfying customers, but the one common denominator is that you're going to have to know what your customers want or need.

At the Home Depot chain, they offer VIP treatment through a "First for Pro" program that targets the contractors, installers, and remodelers who account for 35 percent of their sales. Home Depot lets these customers phone in orders in advance and reserves special parking spots close to the doors for them. They also have staff inside the store dedicated to assisting these customers. Home Depot says that sales to the largest pro customers grew 11 percent after the program was started. This is a classic example of understanding what matters most to the customers and making that what matters most to you.

This raises the bigger question of "How do we find out what our customers want?" You may want data. You may want to hire a company to survey your customers or potential customers to pin down what they want. Get on the Internet and find a customer research firm. They're everywhere. Pick up the phone, call them, and have them come over this afternoon. Write the check and put them to work.

You might want to simply ask your customers yourself through focus groups or customer forums, systematic information gathering, a top-of-mind awareness on the part of employees to always be finding out more about customers, or any number of other ways.

It's not that daunting a task. The hardest part is deciding that determining evolving customer wants and needs on an ongoing basis is a priority, then choosing the approach you wish to take.

The truth is that every business has to satisfy customers just as every business has to make a profit. For some companies, making customer satisfaction what matters most is the most effective driver of strategy.

Quality

Doing quality work is and always has been a cornerstone of what matters most for me in my business. I have always believed that the greatest way to sell our services and create loyalty with customers is to do a great job every single time. In fact, I've been asked how we manage to make my business work without doing any more selling than we do. My answer is that the most effective sales call we can possibly make is to do a great job. Quality creates that most powerful of all marketing forces: word of mouth. In the age of the Internet, word of mouth, especially through social media, has become the great marketing ally of any business that brings true value to the market.

Toyota had built a rock solid reputation and established market leadership by focusing on quality as the thing that mattered most. In 2010, Toyota faced a crisis when reports of acceleration mishaps threw consumer confidence into a tailspin. Eventually, Toyota executives admitted that they had changed their focus from quality to rapid growth, and that this had led to the product problems.

That doesn't mean that a focus on growth as what matters most is wrong for your business. It just means that either it wasn't right for Toyota or that their execution was flawed. And what it means for all of us is that our decision about what matters most is vitally important.

Growth

Despite the cautionary tale from Toyota, it could be that what matters most to your company and its competitive health is growth. Many successful start-ups have chosen growth-focused strategies, and others believe that growth through acquisitions is of primary importance at a particular point in their company's existence. Growth is good. Like anything else, we must be sure that we've chosen the target that will deliver the ultimate result we want.

Why do you want to grow? How do you want to grow? I've known of businesses that measured growth through the number of employees they had. You may want to add a new product or service every year. It could be that there are new markets that you want to enter.

On the other hand, you could achieve a growth in revenue and profit by narrowing your niche and moving out of markets that you are presently in. Sometimes growth doesn't mean more customers or employees. It can mean growing the amount of business you're doing with existing customers or making the decision to devote all of your efforts to one particular market. Think it through. The graveyard of failed companies is haunted with the cries of "What were we thinking?" or "Why did we try to grow so quickly?" or "We should have focused our efforts. We spread ourselves too thin!"

Consistency of Performance

Talk to successful sports coaches, and they will often say that the key to their program's success isn't a focus on winning; it's focusing on process and consistency of performance. The thinking is that if they get the basics right in every practice, then they'll get it right in every game. The consistency will create the wins.

For your business, what might be the greatest performance and profit booster of all is to concentrate on consistency. Consistency of performance is the great brand builder. Inconsistency is the great brand killer. A great aspiration can be "Delivering 90+ percent complete customer satisfaction at every one of our stores." Or you might want to take on "100 percent on-time delivery of product to every customer, every time."

Consider coming up with a list of four things that will ensure your success if you get them right every single time. Of course, the number doesn't have to be four. It can be three or six or whatever fits for you. Don't pick too many, though. As you get beyond a handful of things to focus on, you reach the point of diminishing returns and end up not focusing on anything.

Continuous Improvement

I think that a very strong case can be made that what matters most, no matter what business you're in, is continual improvement. The fact is that if you are constantly improving, you will, by definition, always be innovating and you'll be anticipating and responding to customers' needs in an effective way. Even if continuous improvement isn't what matters most to you, it has to be a core part of how you do business if you are to remain competitive in the market today.

Being Happy, or Creative, or Fulfilled, or . . .

For some people, what matters most isn't a thinking thing; it's a matter of the heart. It's a love thing. Or a creativity thing. It's your call.

The Food Network's show *Diners, Drive-Ins, and Dives* did a feature on a restaurant in Stillwater, Minnesota, called Smalley's Caribbean Barbeque. The owner had worked in fine restaurants in Minneapolis, but he said that what he loved more than anything was making Jamaican barbeque on the weekends with and for his friends.

So he quit his job in Minneapolis and opened Smalley's Caribbean Barbeque. As with most restaurants, it was a case of building it and hoping they would come—which they did. Smalley's was doing a booming business in a small town, serving what many would consider to be some pretty exotic barbeque in a pirate-themed setting.

This is a case of "Here's what I love to do. I think people will pay me to do it." In Smalley's case, it worked.

I have a friend who makes very, very expensive, highest-quality acoustic guitars. The work fulfills him. He believes it is what he is on this planet to do, and happily for him, he's extraordinarily good at it and his work is in demand. He makes a profit. He satisfies his customers. But for him it is the work itself that matters most.

You may want to go with what brings you joy and bliss. Cool. Bliss out. Do what you love, and maybe the money will follow. Just know that if your competition is better at it than you are or if there aren't enough customers willing to pay you to do what brings you joy, then you don't have a business.

For some, the whole love thing is irrelevant to their business. To them, business is business. It's not a love or a passion thing; it's an income thing, and they're in it to make a living. They'll do fun stuff after work and on the weekends. That's fine, too.

Your motivation is whatever it is. Your approach to business may be getting eyebrow deep in data or focusing on nothing but heart and soul. You may be a joy person or a nose to the grindstone person. It's all good.

The Main Thing

The important thing is to think about it, talk about it, stake a claim on what's the most important thing, and get to work on it. Or, as has been said by countless business consultants: The main thing is to make sure the main thing is the main thing. Until you figure out what matters most, it's going to be difficult to know how to organize your time, develop a strategy, and execute tactically.

Questions to Consider

What's a Process You Can Use to Define What's Most Important?

As a starting point for discussion, look at the "what matters most" ideas from this chapter. Think about and discuss each one and how, if at all, it relates to you and your business. Of course, it could be that none of the examples given resonate with you, which is also fine. If they don't, why don't they? What would resonate more?

- Maximize profit.
- Make a positive difference in the world.
- Be number one.
- Satisfy customers.
- Concentrate on quality.
- Grow.
- Achieve consistency of performance.
- Continually improve.
- Be happy, or creative, or fulfilled, or . . .

5

Different Answers— All of Them Right

Wide Open Choices

I could have written a much shorter book and made a lot of people happy if there were one simple answer to what matters the most. How much easier for all of us to just say, "What matters the most is making a profit. Now go forth and prosper."

For most people, this process can be equal parts satisfying and frustrating.

But what ultimately makes it so rewarding is that your choices are wide open. The challenge and opportunity is to simplify and focus on what speaks to your head and your heart, while at the same time being effective in driving the daily activities of you and your team that will sustain and grow the business.

Let's simplify some versions of what matters most for some companies. Although I am numbering the "matters most" items, it's not necessarily in any order of importance. I number them to make the point that it's seldom more than a very small number of things that truly matter most.

Joe Calloway

1. Always put family first.
2. Do quality work.
3. Do work that makes us happy.
4. Always be easy and a pleasure to work with.

I have absolute clarity about what matters most to me. It's my family and creating time to be with them. If my business is working the way it should work, then I'm able to go to the school fair, read books to my first grader's class, and not spend more than a certain number of nights away from home every month. Success for me is now measured in how I spend my time, rather than how much money I make.

"Do quality work" means some very specific things to me. It means make every presentation I give, workshop that I lead, consulting assignment that I do, book that I write, and video that I produce the absolute best it can be. That's where I spend the bulk of my work time. Others in my line of work don't think twice about their presentations. They focus on sales and marketing. Their thinking is that they've already gotten to the point of quality work, so there's no need to constantly tinker with it; that their big priority is selling. We can both be right. They can be right for them. I can be right for me. What matters is whether it works or not and whether it makes you happy.

"Quality work" also means that I'm doing the kind of work that feeds me creatively. I used to get a kick out of speaking to an audience of 10,000 people. I turn down that kind of work today, because what's fun for me is interacting in a conversational way with much smaller audiences. I turn down jobs all the time because they don't fit my personal definition of what would constitute quality work.

"Do work that makes us happy" includes working with and for people who make us happy. No jerks. That's one that has evolved over the years. We have a kind of filter for work and people. There's work that, over time, I have decided I'd simply rather not do because, even though it may be very lucrative, it's not fun anymore. Sometimes when people inquire about working with us, we quickly realize that we don't want to spend time with them. For me, the "life's too short" philosophy carries a lot of weight in deciding what I will and won't spend my time on. Life's too short to do work that I don't enjoy, and life's definitely too short to work with unpleasant people.

Another "what matters most" item for me (and my business partner) is "always be easy and a pleasure to work with." It's a huge part of our brand. It's how we like to do business with people and with each other. It means a thousand things, and we know what those thousand things are. It's in our DNA.

So what's the impact of having figured out what's most important to me? One obvious impact is on how I spend my time every day at work. Take, for example, the time I spend on social media. For lots of people in my profession, social media activity is what matters the most. If that's what drives positive results for them, then they are right. For me, social media activity is something that I do, but never, ever at the expense of putting in the time to be sure I'm doing quality work for my clients.

"Make the quality of the work better" is one of my mantras. I spend the biggest part of my time each day hammering away at every upcoming project, tweaking and changing and improving. It is what matters most to me. That certainly doesn't mean it should to you. But it helps me determine what to do when there's not enough time to do everything (and, of course, there never is). The blog can wait. I do the best I can on the client's project first.

Benjamin Franklin Plumbing

1. Be on time.
2. Clean everything up.
3. Do great work.

I didn't list those in what I think is their order of importance. They are in no particular order. And they are my guess at what's important for Benjamin Franklin Plumbing. Obviously, I can't claim to speak for them. My perspective is as a customer of theirs, as someone who has talked with a lot of their other customers, and as a writer who has done a little research on them.

Their big deal is being on time. Think about it. When you're at home, having taken the afternoon off from work to meet a service person, be it an electrician, a phone technician, a cable company repair person, or a plumber, what's the most irritating thing that can happen? It's when the service person is late.

Now I don't know if Benjamin Franklin Plumbing management hired a research firm to collect data on what customers want when they hire a home service company. Maybe they did. Maybe they have data on top of data that reveal that being late really ticks people off. Or maybe the head of the company just said, "You know what I think? I think if we're always on time and people know that we're always on time, it would get us a ton of business." However they got there, they decided that being on time was one of the things that matters most. My guess is that if you went to any Benjamin Franklin Plumbing location first thing in the morning and asked, "What matters most today?" they would all say, "Being on time."

They also clean up after themselves. They clean up everything or you don't have to pay them. They do it every time because they've decided it's part of what matters most.

Finally, they do very, very good plumbing work. I've always been happy with the quality of their work, as has every one of their customers that I've talked to. Of course, there's no way they have a 100 percent track record of happy customers. No one does. But to a very impressive degree, these guys are on time, they clean everything up, and they do great work.

Wine to Water

1. Provide clean water to needy people around the world.

Wine to Water, a nonprofit organization, was founded by a bartender named Doc Hendley. What I love about Hendley and this organization is not only the remarkably valuable work that they do but also the absolute clarity that they have about what matters the most. I say over and over that if you can make things simple, you can move mountains. Hendley has made the organization's goal and purpose simple, and Wine to Water moves mountains. Find out more at WineToWater.org.

Pinnacle Financial Partners

1. To be the best financial services firm and the best place to work in Tennessee.

I've been writing about Pinnacle Financial Partners for years. I'm a customer of theirs and have experienced firsthand how their focus on a very simple and ambitious vision statement drives quality performance all the way to the customer contact level.

Look again at the two parts of their vision: to be the best financial services firm and the best place to work in Tennessee. This is the kind of goal that for some companies would be just a "feel good" statement that would be taken out at the annual all-employee meeting, read and acknowledged with much applause, and then put back in the drawer for another year. Not so with Pinnacle.

Chief executive officer (CEO) Terry Turner and the rest of the leadership team use their vision statement, along with a clear four-part mission statement and a short set of values, to drive a focused strategy largely based on having clear market targets, providing service and advice, hiring only highly experienced professionals, having a full line of services, and offering "extraordinary convenience."

I've participated in Pinnacle leadership meetings. They've all started with Terry Turner reviewing that two-part vision statement. Then they talk about what they're doing in terms of achieving those goals. It's not subjective. Pinnacle uses a range of measurements to make clear whether or not they are truly making their vision a reality. Their team members buy into the vision (or they wouldn't be there), and everyone knows exactly where they stand in terms of progress and achievement.

Pinnacle is a textbook case of a company in what could be considered a very complicated business, financial services, making it simple, getting clearly focused on what matters the most, and taking action that drives their strategy forward.

Southwest Airlines

1. Great value
2. Excellent service
3. Love and fun

What? Not Southwest Airlines again! Are you sick of reading about Southwest Airlines in almost every book about business that's been written in the past 30 years or so? Well, get used to it. My guess is that we'll be reading about them for another 30 years. They're in the toughest business in the universe, and they make a profit. Read more about Southwest in Chapter 17.

Southwest Airlines has, in my opinion, absolutely nailed the concept of being the best at what matters the most. First and foremost, they want to provide great value. They want to keep fares low. Bags fly free. And they want to give great service, including getting the basics right, such as being on time and having your bags go to the same place you're going.

They also have fun because they hire fun people and it's part of their culture. Having fun is in their DNA, and they don't know any other way to do it. But don't let the fun aspect of Southwest Airlines take away from the fact that these people are laser-focused on creating value and executing with excellence. They know what matters most.

By the way, according to a survey by Buyology Inc. and uSamp, Southwest Airlines was the top brand named among both men and women, making it one of just three brands in the top 10 list for both genders. Let that sink in. In an age where most people who fly frequently would describe the experience as really, really bad, the top brand across all industries in this survey is an airline.

I am frequently interviewed about business success and often asked to name a company that I think gets it right. Southwest Airlines is at the top of my list. I believe that the single most important key to their sustained success is an absolute clarity about what matters most and a devotion to executing on those things with quality and consistency.

An Advertising Agency That I Read about Many Years Ago

1. Do great work.
2. Have fun.

3. Make money.
4. Don't work with people you can't stand.

I don't remember the name of the company. I just know that it must have been at least 25 years ago that I read about them and I still remember their list of what matters most.

What struck me as being so powerful about their list was that they put it into words that must have felt right to them. I don't get the sense that they hired a consultant to come up with a proper sounding vision or mission statement. They just looked at each other and said, "Okay. What's important? How are we going to do this thing?"

Whenever I share this list with people, there's usually someone who says, "Can they really do that? Can they say stuff like 'Don't work with people you can't stand'?" Hey, it's their company. They can say whatever they like and say it however they like. If they try to sound like they think they're supposed to or like they think the CorporateSpeak Police would want them to sound, then it will be useless anyway.

This is a great lesson in giving real, gut-level power to your list of what matters most. It has to be in your voice. It has to strike a chord, an emotional chord, with you, not with anyone else. Your list of what matters most should turn you on. You might have a pocket protector full of pens and markers and what turns you on would be something like "We solve the toughest physics problems in the world." For someone else, what matters most could be "We absolutely rock at making doughnuts."

Say it the way you think it. The way you say it should matter to you. You're not doing this for a grade. You're doing it to make the right things happen. This is about effectiveness, not etiquette.

Somebody at Citi Cards

1. Make the statement easier to read and use.

I just got an e-mail from Citi Cards (I'm a cardholder) that says that after a lot of customer feedback, they are coming out with a new, easier-to-read, easier-to-use monthly statement. For somebody at Citi Cards, what mattered the most was changing the statement. To whoever they are, I say thank you.

Obviously, I'm not saying that making the statement easier to read and use is what matters most to the entire company. Citi's corporate mission statement is, in part, to try to create the best outcomes for customers through financial solutions. As that declaration of what matters most filtered down to various departments and people within the company, it translated to someone as taking action on improving the statement. Evidently, that person had been getting feedback from customers about what worked and didn't work on the statement and made the appropriate changes.

This is a perfect example of going from a general statement of what matters the most, creating best outcomes for customers, down to the specific action on what matters the most, making changes in the statement.

What Fits Us Best?

Does deciding what matters the most take the place of our vision statement or mission statement? Are we deciding what matters the most forever? For right now? Should we take a big-picture approach like a focus on profit or customer satisfaction, or should we focus on something specific, such as being on time every time?

We could come up with 100 questions like these, so let me answer all of them with this: whatever you think will work best for you. That's not a cop-out. That's the way it works. You have to take responsibility for deciding what approach fits you best or fits your organization best. More on this in Chapter 21.

Does the CEO decide what matters most? Does the owner or the board of directors? Is this a group process? Do we turn it over to our customers and let them tell us what's most important?

Whatever you think will work best for you.

There are consultants that will tell you that your decisions and priorities should be driven by customer focus groups. In an interview with *Business Week,* Steve Jobs of Apple said, "It's really hard to design products by focus groups. A lot of times, people don't know what they want until you show it to them." Jobs was famous for designing and releasing the products that he personally thought would be successful. Was Jobs wrong to take such a "whatever you think will work best for you" approach? Hardly.

It's Worth Doing Wrong

So there you have it—some food for thought. Now the hard work is to determine for yourself what matters most to you. Don't get hung up on getting it exactly right or avoid starting because you can't pick from the 30 or 40 things that you think could all qualify for the list. Pick three or four. Better yet, pick one, such as "satisfy the customer" or "maximize profit."

One thing's for sure. If you don't begin, you'll never get there. As my friend Arnie Malham, CEO of cj Advertising says, "If it's worth doing, it's worth doing wrong. If you wait for everything to be perfect, you'll never do it, and then it's an opportunity lost. Do it. Do it wrong. Then do it better."

Questions to Consider

Looking at the preceding examples and how each company approaches what matters most, what do you like and not like about each? There is no right or wrong here. But use the examples to start a discussion about what three or four things matter most to you and your team.

- Joe Calloway
- Benjamin Franklin Plumbing
- Wine to Water
- Pinnacle Financial Partners
- Southwest Airlines
- The advertising agency
- Citi Cards

6

Relevance, Innovation, and Constant Improvement

A Moving Target

It goes without saying, but I'll say it again anyway so that it doesn't get lost in our discussion about being the best: Being the best is a moving target. Being the best means that you have to be relevant. If you think being the best means getting really great at something and stopping, then you will have been the best yesterday but today you'll be out of business.

There is no need for me to waste a lot of time telling you why we all have to constantly change, innovate, and improve. We all know it, and it's in every business book ever written. Let's talk about whether we're any good at change, and if not, what mind-set can make us better.

Better Tomorrow Than You Were Today

When I work with a group, I always ask, "In order for you to stay competitive, do you have to be better tomorrow than you were today?" The responses I get are nearly unanimous. Everyone agrees that they have to improve every single day if they are to survive, much less grow their businesses.

I then ask a much tougher follow-up question: "What did you do last Wednesday that made you better than you were on Tuesday?" That's when I lose eye contact, and everyone begins to think, "Well, let's see. Last Wednesday was really busy. We were slammed and had all we could handle just staying on top of everything. There's no way we could really think about improving last Wednesday."

Lip Service

No idea gets more lip service than the idea of constant improvement. But if you buy into this idea of being the best at what matters most, it's not an option. You cannot be considered the best at anything and you can't say that you are doing your best unless you are relevant. And to be relevant, you have to continually improve, not as occasional improvement projects, but as an integral part of how you do what you do every single day.

Many people fail to improve and innovate because they think they aren't creative enough. Let go of thinking that innovation is something that takes a wildly creative mind. Innovation is simply taking an existing idea and adapting it to what you do to make something better. The need to improve and innovate is a theme woven through the very core of being the best at what matters the most.

To actually win, and keep winning on the basics, you have to innovate like crazy. You have to improve relentlessly. But you must innovate and improve where you'll realize the greatest return on your efforts. Get better at the things that create the greatest value for the customer. You should constantly innovate and improve on those three or four things that matter the most. If you do that, your product or service will be continually evolving and you'll be leaving your competitors in your dust.

Improve Constantly and Forever

A few years ago I became interested in the work of William Edwards Deming, who came to be known as the father of the total quality management movement. His book *Out of the Crisis* is, in my opinion, one of the top two or three books ever written on business. And in that book he introduced his famous 14 points for management.

I encourage you to hop on the Internet and find Deming's 14 points for management. Some of those ideas were, and still are, considered not only groundbreaking but quite contrarian.

Take, for example, this one: "Cease dependence on inspection to achieve quality. Eliminate the need for massive inspection by building quality into the product in the first place."

What? Stop inspecting for quality? Most managers in manufacturing had to read that one over and over to let it sink in. Deming helped countless businesses rethink and redefine what they did and how they did it.

The idea that Deming championed, perhaps above all others, was the idea of continual improvement. The first of Deming's 14 points for management is to "Create constancy of purpose toward improvement of product and service, with the aim to become competitive, stay in business and to provide jobs." Point number five is to "Improve constantly and forever the system of production and service, to improve quality and productivity, and thus constantly decrease costs."

"Create constancy of purpose toward improvement" and "improve constantly and forever." These two phrases have been the foundation for what I believe drives success in business or any other endeavor. The one thing that I would imagine that every reader of this book has in common is that all of us believe we can do better.

Questions to Consider

- What are you doing in your business today that will be irrelevant two years from now?
- What are the three things that you have to do now to stay relevant to your customers?
- What are the three things that you have to do now to become relevant to the customers that you wish you were doing business with?

7

Culture, Focus, and More Focus

Memphis Invest

A Little Company with Powerful Lessons

This is a story with powerful lessons for anyone who wants to harness the power of being the best at what matters the most. After 30 years of working with some of the best companies and organizations in the world, it takes a lot to impress me. This little company in Memphis, Tennessee, absolutely knocks my socks off.

Memphis Invest is a family business founded by Kent Clothier, Sr., in 2004, and it has grown into a multigenerational family-owned business that provides real estate investment opportunities in both the Memphis and Dallas markets. Kent's sons, Brett, Chris, and Kent, Jr., lead the management team. The company manages all phases of the investment process on behalf of its investors, from property acquisition to renovation and tenant management. Their goal is to maximize their clients' investment dollars and minimize risk while providing positive cash flow, tax benefits, and "peace of mind investing" for all of their clients, who are located throughout the United States and around the world.

Memphis Invest was recognized as Business of the Year in their local community in 2012, and it was nominated for Small Business of the Year by the *Memphis Business Journal*.

Get the Fundamentals Right

To me, this statement on its website sums up the company's thinking about the business: "Solid fundamentals lead to cash flow." This is the attitude that the Clothiers and all of their employees have toward their business: Get the fundamentals right. These guys have mastered being the best at what matters most through simplicity, focus, and action.

At Memphis Invest, they've made it simple. What matters the most are the fundamentals of real estate investing and the fundamentals of great customer service. That's it. Two things to think about. But they think about those two things all the time. It drives their priorities and keeps them laser focused on flawless execution.

Early on in researching the company, I asked Chris Clothier to send me whatever information he thought was most important for me to know about the company. He sent me the same thing that he sends to prospective clients, *The Memphis Invest Culture Book.*

The Culture Book

Here is how Memphis Invest describes its culture book:

> Our culture book is loaded with pages and pages of pictures from events around the country as well as testimonials from employees, vendors, clients and partners. This is NOT a marketing book. There is nothing in here on the market itself or how great the returns can be. No space is wasted trying to convince everyone on why Memphis or Dallas are the right market for investors. There is plenty of material showing those stats. This is all about what we think makes our great company, well . . . GREAT!"

What is most impressive about the culture book is that Memphis Invest let the staff tell the story of what matters most in their own words. Here are some excerpts from the culture book in the words of the Memphis Invest staff talking about the customer focus aspect of their culture:

> I love that the company is client focused, which removes all of the red tape and allows me to make decisions based on what is best for the client.

> I love the motto of putting customer service first, and I believe that the entire company makes that their mission every day.

> The environment here at Memphis Invest promotes its employees to not be afraid to be different with the common goal of ultimate customer satisfaction.

> The one thing everyone has in common is the focus on getting results and providing great service.

> We care about our investors. We care about their properties. We care about their success.

> Above all other there is a premium placed on loyalty, both to each other, and to our clients.

> Usually in real estate it's location, location, location. For us it's service, service, service, and not just service—the BEST service.

You get the point. Although there are many aspects to the Memphis Invest culture, when you talk with the employees there, it's obvious that a focus on the customer is a core value, and it drives everything that they do.

I interviewed Chris Clothier, Director of Sales and Marketing and a partner in the company, about how Memphis Invest stays focused on what matters most.

A Handful of Numbers

Joe: The premise of "Be the best at what matters most" is that successful companies have real clarity and focus on the handful of things that really matter—those things that they must do really well every single day. I'm impressed by how everyone at Memphis Invest seems to have clarity on what the priorities are, who's responsible for what, and what has to be done every single day. As a leader in the company, tell me how you think about this idea of staying focused on the important things, and how you've managed to do such a great job of that with your team.

Chris: I was taught early on that, in business, you can judge the health of your business by measuring a handful of numbers each day. For us, there are a few numbers we track daily from each of our departments, and they are not all geared toward financial numbers either. We do watch account balances, but we are much more focused on being aware of smaller detail numbers. Data such as the number of late payments, the number of customer experience calls completed, the number of new leads connected with, the number of days to complete renovations, average dollars spent on renovations, how many rental applications were completed, and, most important, whether there were any complaints the day before. These are just a few of the numbers we can look at daily and compare with a historical record; we can judge the health of our company and if there is an area that we may need to focus energy or a particular problem developing that we can address early.

We have department heads who lead each of the departments, and it is their responsibility to be in all of the numbers at a much deeper level. We meet a minimum of once a week with all department heads and often twice a week for a few minutes to go through the details of their departments and let them update us on trends they are seeing and get their opinion on issues we need to address. This empowers our people and begins to teach them to quickly identify the direction of their departments and dig into the numbers deeper when there are issues.

Absolute Intention and Focus

I had the opportunity to attend the early morning meetings of each of the departments at Memphis Invest. I was extremely impressed with the absolute intention and focus of every single participant in these meetings. Everyone knew exactly what was to be covered at the meeting, the metrics to be reviewed, the problems to be solved, and, possibly most important, who was accountable for every single action to be taken following the meeting.

It's fascinating to me that just the way these meetings were conducted spoke volumes about how this company knows exactly what matters most and is thus able to prioritize activities so effectively. Founder Kent Clothier made clear in these meetings when he was not satisfied with any aspect of the team's performance, and he made very clear that everyone was 100 percent accountable for producing results. He did this in a way that was both demanding and supportive.

Clarity about Expectations

I think that a key driver of the high effectiveness level in the company is their absolute clarity about what is expected. Here are some employee comments from the culture book about expectations and results at Memphis Invest:

The two most important pieces of our culture are "work ethic" and "attitude." Hard work is rewarded. We do not cut corners and lazy work will be exposed. There is an attitude between everyone at the company that this is THE best place to work and we are THE best at what we do.

It's everyone doing their job and whatever needs to be done to keep moving forward.

Kent Clothier is a hard man to work for. He demands more from you than even you yourself think you can accomplish. That's why at the end of the day you're amazed at what you can accomplish in life with a great leader.

The business culture at Memphis Invest is based on results, first and foremost.

I like that they expect you to do more. Not to expect much from people is demeaning. Not to want your best is unimaginative. The people here are pushed to be the best and use their imaginations and that feels great.

Mediocrity is not acceptable. When you have a leader that wants to reach one step higher, it is an incentive for his staff to better themselves.

The culture to me is based on us having a positive mindset that anything is possible with the proper planning.

Meetings as Opportunities

I continued my interview with Chris Clothier by asking him about these meetings that made such a powerful impression on me.

Joe: Your meetings are extremely focused, efficient, and effective. Talk about your philosophy about the purpose of meetings and how they should be conducted.

Chris: First, we do not especially like meetings but recognize the absolute necessity to keep everyone on the same page and fully informed. Meetings are often our opportunity to continue teaching not only leaders but any staff members present our business operational philosophy. We have found that keeping people informed, providing a forum for feedback, and being transparent with the direction we as owners want to go builds a strong team, and that is what we have. Meetings are not opportunities to make speeches; they are designed to get information, ideas, and directions out to everyone quickly and that is what we look to do. They are also a great tool to develop leaders from within, so we readily turn over the reins of our meetings to the leaders in our company, which helps to build that team spirit.

Relationships That Wow

Chris and I also talked about their focus on customer relationships, which is a thread woven through everything that they do.

Joe: One thing that obviously matters most to your success is the relationship that you have with your clients. Feel free to tell me anything you want about the Memphis Invest philosophy of building extraordinary relationships with clients.

Chris: As in any relationship, the only way to grow a strong bond is through sincerity, authenticity, and continuous opportunity for growth. So we consider those important factors in everything we do, from personal e-mails, e-mail newsletters, personal thank-you cards, personal phone calls to invitations to join us for special events both in Memphis and near where clients and potential clients live. Before investors ever become clients, we hope that they get a sense that we are a different type of company.

We want them to get a sense that we really do care about building a long-term relationship that is beneficial both for them as a client and us as a service provider. We send a handwritten, personal thank-you card to every single person who registers for more information on our company. We always address e-mail contact with everyone registering at our website in a personal manner and make all of those e-mails educational in nature so that they can take as much time as needed to get to know us. Every person who registers receives a personal phone call just to see if they have any questions about the company.

These initial touches are so important because they set the tone for those investors who eventually buy homes and become clients with us. After they become clients, we have an entire department committed to customer service. They contact every client every month by phone and ask one simple question: What can we do for you? Even though that department is all about serving our clients, we teach customer service every week in our staff meetings so that every phone call, every e-mail, every personal contact with a client, regardless of who they interact with at the company, ends with the client saying "wow." That is the focus of our company.

One thing I often warn my clients about is not to be distracted by chasing wow factors through gimmicks. Memphis Invest creates wow factors in the only way that really counts: through extraordinary performance and service for their clients.

Memphis Invest is a model in terms of how simplicity and a focus on what matters most can create positive results for the company, the employees, and the customers.

Questions to Consider

- Does every single person in your organization have absolute clarity of focus about what is most important for them to accomplish in their jobs every single day?
- Do you?
- On a scale of 1 to 10, how clear are expectations in your organization?
- Do you accept mediocrity, or do you demand excellence from yourself and everyone on the team?
- If you say that you exceed your customers' expectations, what are the examples of you doing that?
- If I asked the people on your team if this is the best job they've ever had, what would they say?

8

Working in the Business

Thinking When You Should Be Working

Your business card isn't what matters the most. Neither is your logo or your mission statement. Sometimes it's easy to get lost in thinking about your business when what you should be doing is "working in" your business.

A blog that I regularly read is *The Entrepreneurial Mind* (drjeffcornwall.com), by Dr. Jeff Cornwall, Massey Chair in Entrepreneurship and director of the Center for Entrepreneurship at Belmont University in Nashville, Tennessee. Dr. Cornwall has a way of cutting through the noise around business and getting to the heart of the matter. I thought that one of his recent columns had particular relevance to the idea of being the best at what matters the most.

"When It Is Time to Work in Your Business," by Dr. Jeff Cornwall

Here is a sampling of quotes from first-time entrepreneurs that I hear in my office.

"I am trying to get my business card just right—does it look better with a horizontal layout or a vertical one? And do you think this font is OK?"

"We think that after working on it for the past six months that our business plan is just about finished."

"I've been tweaking my logo for the past couple of weeks and I think it is getting close to what I want."

"This is my latest mission statement—I moved a couple of words around so I hope it sounds better now."

It is as if they are planning a dinner party and spent all their time worrying about getting the centerpiece and place settings just right, but forgot that they need to plan a meal to serve their guests.

Entrepreneurs who own growing ventures will inevitably hear that they need to stop working "in the business" and start working "on the business." With many first-time entrepreneurs, I see them making the opposite mistake.

Even before they generate their first dollar of revenue, many seem obsessed with working "on the business."

It often seems as if they aren't able to pull the trigger and actually launch the business.

Here are a few tips for first-time entrepreneurs who suffer from this common condition:

1. While a well-designed business card is nice to have, it is you and your product or service that will persuade customers to spend hard-earned money on what you have to offer them.

2. Your actual product will rarely look anything like what you may envision in a business plan. In fact, unless you are looking to raise a large amount of capital from outside investors or bankers, writing a formal business plan is not even necessary. Customers will provide feedback that should inform and shape the new business in its early stages of growth. Real information from actual customers is much more important than guesses made in a formal business plan.

3. A cool-looking logo may be nice to have at some point, but a logo is just a symbol that represents a business. Get the business going, then worry about a logo to help people remember who you are.

4. Most mission statements I read are ambiguous and tell very little about what a business really does.

Work on a simple, memorable pitch that will help customers know exactly what you can offer them.

Unless you are able to muster the courage, and get out and "work in" your new business, things like business cards, logos and business plans have no value. While getting a new business going, your job is not to design the perfect image and develop the perfect business plan; it is to find customers and sell them your product.

Without customers to generate revenues, there really is no business to "work on." So step away from your computer and go find some real live customers.

Questions to Consider

- What are the nuts and bolts of your business that you have been neglecting?
- What do you need to do right now to find more customers?
- What existing customers do you need to contact immediately?
- What will you do to increase business with your existing customers?
- What do you need to ask your customers right now?

9

Three Is the Magic Number

Smile Brands

These Three Things

These guys have got knowing what matters the most figured out. They simplify. They focus. They act.

Smile Brands Group, Inc., is the largest provider of support services to general and multispeciality dental groups in the United States based on number of dental offices. The company handles the administrative, marketing, and financial aspects of a dental practice, allowing the dentists to spend more time caring for patients.

I worked with Smile Brands at two events, one for the managers of dental practices and the other for dentists. What impressed me so much was the focus on what Smile Brands calls its G3 Service Platform. With this model, Smile Brands has narrowed down what matters the most in fulfilling its mission—"deliver smiles to everyone"—to three components: "Greeting. Guiding. Gratitude."

I've worked with companies that expected team members to remember:

- The vision
- The mission
- The 10 values
- The 12 "pillars of our brand"
- The 7 "differences we make"
- The 9 "ways we succeed"

And on and on. It's ridiculous and ends up being white noise and nothing more than distractions that serve to confuse priorities, not establish them.

Pick a Lane

At Smile Brands, managers have picked a lane with just three things to focus on. They say that greeting, guiding, and gratitude are how they express their passion and respect for everyone they touch. They are intended to be expressed by team members not only with patients but with one another as well.

Remember in the opening chapter of this book, I quoted Steve Jobs as saying that it takes a lot of hard work to "get your thinking clean enough to make things simple." The G3 Service Platform is a perfect example of how Smile Brands has done just that.

The G3 Approach

The short version of the three components of the G3 Service Platform is:

Greeting: Give a warm, sincere greeting to everyone you meet.
Guiding: Explain to each patient what's going to happen, why it's necessary, and how you will be helping him or her.
Gratitude: Thank every person you interact with for the privilege of serving him or her.

The Power of Simplicity

When I worked with Smile Brands on its events, the power of the company's focus on the G3 Service Platform was evident. I didn't have to blend my work with 25 different initiatives from Smile Brands' side. All I had to do was help the managers make an already effective strategy even more effective. The simplicity of the company's approach made it easy for everyone to focus on how to improve and innovate within the G3 Service Platform.

Unifying a team around a shared purpose and empowering them to improve their performance around that purpose becomes infinitely easier when the objectives are simple. Look again at the components of the G3 Service Platform: Greeting, Guiding, and Gratitude. If everyone on a Smile Brands team can become the best at those three things, then their success is ensured.

The Ultimate Sophistication

"That won't work. It's too simple. This is a complicated business." It's so much easier to take refuge in the defense that things are just too complicated than it is to actually do anything about them. Many people prefer to keep having more meetings and just talk about their challenges rather than take action on simple solutions or strategies.

To those who say, "It's not that simple," I say, "Yes. It usually *is* that simple. But it takes a willingness to do the hard work of simplification, focus, and action that most people don't have." Some believe that taking a complicated view of things shows their sophistication. I refer them to Leonardo da Vinci, who said, "Simplicity is the ultimate sophistication."

So Much Less Effort

It is a pleasure to work with people like chief executive officer Steve Bilt and his leadership team at Smile Brands. There's so much less effort required because they were willing to do the hard work up front to simplify their strategy. Once you "go simple" and see how it lets you focus clearly—which enables you to take action more effectively—you'll never go back to complicated again.

Questions to Consider

- On a scale of 1 to 10, how well does everyone on a our team understand exactly what is expected of them?
- Have you made expectations simple or complicated?
- What are the three things that everyone on your team should always do with every customer?
- What are the three things that everyone on your team should always do with everyone else on your team?

10

Winning and Losing Inside the Box

There Aren't Any Shortcuts

In a tough market, it's tempting to look for shortcuts. Reality check: There aren't any shortcuts. The one business strategy that creates and sustains success is to be the best at what matters the most. What an audacious idea—outperform your competition on those things that create real value for your customer.

Deliver on Your Promise Every Time

One of the most popular concepts in business over the past 10 years has been the wow factor. It seems that everyone's focused on surprising the customer with something different. That's all well and good, but understand that the ultimate and most powerful wow factor is to deliver on your promise every time, with every customer, with amazing consistency.

They've Taken Their Eyes Off the Ball

For years, we've all talked about the need to think outside the box. I take that to mean that we need to be open to new ideas, new ways of doing things, innovation, and creative thinking. I'm for it. Count me in.

The trap that many have fallen into, however, is being so enamored of the idea of thinking outside the box that they've taken their eyes off the ball. They've started spending so much time outside the box that they're losing the battle where it's being fought, which is squarely inside the box.

If You Win on the Basics, You Win It All

Let me explain what I mean. You want to constantly innovate and improve for one purpose: to win inside the box. By "inside the box," I mean those things that matter most to the market-place. These are the basic expectations of your customers. These are the things that your customers value most. I go back to my core premise, which is that if you can clearly win on those basics, you win it all. It's how every market leader succeeds.

Throughout this book there are examples of companies that win inside the box. I use that term to get your attention and to challenge the idea that the more out there the idea is, the better it is. It's not about how outside the box your idea is; it's about how useful and effective your idea is. Sometimes that can be something you come up with that's radically different and edgy. Great. Go for it. The bottom line test, however, is how your idea affects the bottom line.

In many ways, the thinking in this book is radically contrarian. It seems that the conventional wisdom in business today, and what we hear from business authors, speakers, and consultants, is that, above all, you must be unique. They say that to compete and win you should focus your efforts on being different and doing things that absolutely none of your competitors is doing. They back these ideas up by telling really cool stories about really cool companies.

Barneys versus Nordstrom

A couple of years ago, I heard a marketing consultant tell his audience that they should emulate Barneys New York because it was the hip, edgy wave of the future in retailing. His example of the kind of business model to avoid was tired old Nordstrom. He said that Nordstrom was, in effect, a dinosaur of retailing and simply wasn't cool enough to survive.

Fast-forward to today. Nordstrom is booming, and the *Wall Street Journal* recently reported that oh-so-cool Barneys

New York "skirts bankruptcy." You know what's cooler than Barneys New York? Making a profit and staying in business.

Don't get me wrong. I'm not saying that being hip, cool, and edgy won't work. It may be exactly what you need to do to be the best at what matters most. My point is that all around us are books and articles and speakers and experts who are telling us that to succeed in business today, we have to do the unexpected, the unique, and the outrageous. What I'm saying, based on the facts of who is winning and who is losing in the marketplace, is that you win not by being the most unique but by being the best. Imagine that.

It's a Sucker's Game

So beware of anyone who says that the key to winning in this market is to focus on being different through over-the-top acts of uniqueness. It's a wild goose chase. It's a sucker's game. It will throw you off course. The best way to be different is to be demonstrably better than your competition at the basics, at what matters the most to customers. Don't agree? Read on. The evidence today is overwhelmingly on the side of quality performance as the only sustainable success strategy.

I'll Happily Take the Doughnut

But, Joe, what about pleasantly surprising the customer? Sure. Bring it on. Give me a doughnut the next time I'm at the bank. Run out to my car with an umbrella when it's raining. I love it. But what I love even more is for you to do your job the right way every single time. That doesn't mean that consistency and giving something extra are mutually exclusive. Of course they're not.

What it does mean is that you should take another look at the basics of your business and be sure that you are hitting 10 on a scale of 1 to 10 inside the box before you start thinking about how you can surprise your customers.

Your "Table Stakes" Aren't Working

I had a bank client once tell me that good service for customers in the branches was just table stakes and that they were interested in playing above that level. I did a little mystery shopping and visited 12 of their branches. I just walked in and waited in the center of the branch. In 8 of the branches, it took more than 5 minutes before anyone even asked if I needed help.

Going beyond table stakes is all well and good, but if you are lousy at the table stakes, then you'd better focus there before you start thinking up what cool little surprises you can offer to win business. The battle is won and lost inside the box.

The new reality in business today is that quality and consistency rule. Hype and gimmicks are dead. The Internet and an infinitely more sophisticated and informed breed of customer killed them. More to come on how the Internet killed hype, but in a nutshell, if a business is all hype and can't deliver the goods, the word that "the emperor has no clothes" gets out at the speed of a few strokes of the keyboard. You can't fool any of the people any of the time anymore, because they're online busting poorly performing companies right and left.

Bells and Whistles Wear Off

37signals develops Web-based collaboration apps for small businesses. Its mantra is "Bells and whistles wear off, but usefulness never does." What matters the most to 37signals is quality, usefulness, and attention to detail.

37signals is a cutting-edge, incredibly cool company. That's nice. What's nicer is that it is a very, very good company that succeeds. It's an example of a business that uses innovative thinking to win inside the box.

Glitz or Profit?

It takes real determination and perseverance to simplify your business, get focused on what matters the most, and be the best. It's not easy. The fact is that most people can't do or won't do what I'm advising you to do. It's much easier, albeit much less profitable, to pursue the glitz of gimmicks that will supposedly set you apart.

But the huge payoff for your effort comes when you begin to make being the best at what matters most your natural way of doing things. Then it does make work and life easier. You'll reach the point where you look at your business and think, Why didn't I always do it this way? It changes everything.

Questions to Consider

- What are your customers' three or four most basic expectations?
- What do your customers value most from you?
- Are you better on the basics than your competition?
- What would you have to do to improve your performance on those basics by 10 percent?
- Thinking outside the box is essential, but what is your purpose for doing so?
- On a scale of 1 to 10, how useful are you to your customers?

11

Random versus Consistent

What a Wonderful Story!

A customer service expert tells a wonderful story about a random act of wow by a restaurant chain. She was extolling the virtues of this restaurant, and the story in her own words, was about, "how they treat their customers."

It seems that a young woman was sick and confined to her bed at home. On Facebook the young woman posted about her sad condition and said that the one thing that she was craving was a particular dish from this particular restaurant.

One of the employees of the restaurant happened to see the Facebook post. She showed it to her manager, who told the staff to pack up the woman's favorite dish and take it to her. What a wonderful story! It truly is a fabulous random act of wow.

That's the Trap

But it's *not* how that restaurant treats its customers. It's how the restaurant treated one customer on one day when it did something special. You see, that's the trap. We get all excited over some out-of-the-ordinary thing that we do, or a story about something that a superstar employee does, and we say that's our standard of performance.

Somebody stop the madness! It's great that this restaurant took the surprise meal to the sick woman. Yay! The people there are to be congratulated. But it's not by any stretch of the imagination how those same people treat their customers in any meaningful way.

Regular, Everyday Customers

If you want to know how they really treat their customers, then you need to find out what their regular, everyday customers think about:

- The quality of the food
- The price
- How long people have to wait to be seated
- How long people have to wait to get their food
- Whether or not the staff is efficient, effective, and nice to do business with
- Whether the food is hot when it's brought to the table
- How easy it is to park
- How long people have to wait to pick up take-out orders
- Every other basic thing that the restaurant does every day with every single customer

I'm beating this point into the ground because it's the point that so many businesses miss. Random acts of wow are wonderful. Do them. But that's not where you'll win or lose the game. Don't think that some once-a-year special thing that you do ever takes the place of consistently being the best at what matters most.

If You Lose Inside the Box

Put your energy, effort, and focus into doing a really, really great job on the basics and into consistency of performance. That determines how you treat your customers. Then be on the lookout for the sick customer who you can surprise with a free meal. Jump all over it.

Unless . . . unless having an employee leave the restaurant to deliver this wow meal leaves the rest of the staff short-handed, meaning the regular everyday customers have to wait longer for their meals because of it. Then all you've got is one happy, special customer, and a restaurant full of customers who are angry and waiting for their food.

If you lose inside the box, you lose.

Questions to Consider

If I ask which of your team members would provide excellent customer-focused performance, who would you suggest? Would the answer be "all of them"? If not, why not?

- For restaurants, the list of relevant factors in terms of how you treat your customers every single day might look like the list from earlier in this chapter:
    - The quality of the food
    - The price
    - How long people have to wait to be seated
    - How long people have to wait to get their food
    - Whether or not the staff is efficient, effective, and nice to do business with
    - Whether the food is hot when it's brought to the table
    - How easy it is to park
    - How long people have to wait to pick up take-out orders

- And every other basic thing that the restaurant does every day with every single customer

What would the list look like for your business, and how would you rank your performance in each category?

12

Simplicity and the Blue-Tip Flame

You Can Move Mountains

Simple is more powerful and more effective than complicated. As I pointed out in Chapter 1, Steve Jobs said his philosophy was that you have to work hard to get your thinking clean enough to make things simple but that it's worth the effort, because if you can make things simple, you can move mountains.

That's worth repeating: If you can make things simple, you can move mountains.

The more complicated you've made your business, the less effective you will be. Complication freezes you into uncertainty and inaction. Simplicity enables you to get everyone focused on a shared vision, goal, or priorities and move forward. It's extremely hard for anyone, much less an entire organization, to focus on anything that's complicated. There is incredible power in simplicity.

What You Need Is a Force Multiplier

You don't have all the time in the world, nor do you have unlimited money or people. You may have a one-person business, in which case you're all you've got. To win with finite resources requires that you leverage every single resource at your disposal. What you need is a force multiplier.

Force multiplier is a military term that is the effect produced by a capability that, when added to and employed by a combat force, significantly increases the combat potential of that force and thus enhances the probability of the mission being successfully accomplished.

Colin Powell said, "Perpetual optimism is a force multiplier." I like that idea, and I agree with former Secretary of

State Powell. I believe is that optimism comes from success and that success comes from simplicity and focus.

Simplicity and focus are your force multipliers.

Get Your Thinking Clean Enough

The great challenge is, as Steve Jobs said, to "get your thinking clean enough to make things simple." It's so much easier to come up with 20 priorities than it is to come up with 3 priorities. The obvious problem with 20 priorities is that it's a bogus concept. You can't focus on everything. Having 20 priorities means having no priorities.

Whether it's your vision, your mission, or your goals for the year, make it all 20 words or less. Write it so that a fifth grader can understand it.

Henry David Thoreau said, "Our life is frittered away by detail. Simplify, simplify, simplify. I say, let your affairs be as two or three, and not a hundred or a thousand; instead of a million count half a dozen, and keep your accounts on your thumb nail."

Blue–Tip Flame

I go back to my analogy of the flamethrower versus the blue-tip flame from an acetylene torch. Peter Sheahan uses this comparison to great effect in his book *Making It Happen*.

If you blast a steel wall with the relatively large flame of a flamethrower, you'll create a lot of heat but you won't get through the wall. If, however, you use the blue-tip flame from an acetylene torch, you can cut through the steel like it is butter.

Some people immediately reject the blue-tip flame philosophy. They will refuse to believe that the success of extraordinary companies and top performers is driven by a mind-set and strategy of clarity and focus. It may even make some people angry, because it will be considered radically contrarian and fly in the face of many of today's most popular business writers and gurus who say we must do a thousand things in the interest of being different.

Remember, top performers aren't the people who do the most things. Top performers are the people who do the most important things.

Questions to Consider

- Where have we made our business too complicated?
- What is something we can do immediately, right now, to simplify things?
- What do we need to stop doing?
- What are three things that we need to take off our list and let go of for now?
- Where do we need to apply a blue-tip flame?

13
The Trap
Let's Do More

Better Is Better

How can we make our business better? Maybe the best answer to that question is to not look for something else to do but to do a better job on what you're already doing. We get so caught up in the idea that more is better that we lose sight of the absolute truth that, no, actually better is better. Looking for more extras to add and cherries to put on top can actually be counterproductive. Stay focused.

Lost in Trying to Be the Best

Michael Heard is a former minister, therapist, and stand-up comedian. More to the point, Heard is one of the best business thinkers I know. He is a principal of 3 Big Questions, a consultancy that "helps organizations triage, stabilize, and prioritize action plans through facilitation and conflict resolution services."

Heard told me a story of one of his clients who fell into the trap of looking beyond what mattered the most in their well-intentioned efforts to do more. I asked him to share that story:

> Being the best at what matters most is sometimes lost in the effort to simply be the best. Case in point. A hospital I was working with had achieved phenomenal success in improving their patient satisfaction in a rather rapid period of time. Over a period of three years, they had improved their patient satisfaction scores from the low 40 percent mark to the middle 90 percent range, placing them not only in the top quartile but in the top 10 percent of high scores in the country.

They worked hard to achieve this success and felt confident they could continue to improve their progress. So they set a goal to reach and achieve the top patient satisfaction scores in the country. More specifically, they wanted to score above 97 percent in all areas of patient satisfaction. They wanted to be the best!

Once they focused on the goal of being the best, a strange thing happened. Their scores starting dropping. All of a sudden their scores dropped to the low 70s, and nothing they seem to do could help them reverse the trend. The perplexed [chief executive officer] asked if I could help them figure out what was going on.

Now, I had no experience (at the time) in the science and art of improving patient satisfaction. My work was in assisting the hospital to develop its strategic plan. None-theless I agreed to help. I reviewed [the hospital's] history and training processes, talked to many individuals at different levels in the organization, and came to a simple conclusion. The organization had lost sight of "what matters most."

The goal of achieving the highest patient satisfaction scores possible caused their focus to shift. The focus shifted to reducing the negative rather than growing the positive.

Any negative comment or less-than-perfect patient experience required an immediate and "calibrated" response. And before long, the development and imple-mentation of these calibrated responses replaced all the basic "blocking and tackling" activities of creating posi-tive patient experiences.

My recommendation was [the hospital needed] to return its focus to concentrating on the basics of its tried-and-true (basic blocking and tackling) approach to creating positive patient satisfaction experiences. To emphasize this point I shared a piece of advice given to me when I was learning stand-up comedy: "Never play to the one table not laughing, or you will lose the rest of the crowd."

They took the recommendation, and their scores returned to the low to middle 90 percent range. To my knowledge they never have achieved the best overall patient satisfaction scores in the country, but their consistent continuing focus on growing the positive has resulted in consistently high patient satisfaction scores ever since. In other words, they figured how to do the best in regard to what mattered most.

I relate this experience and lessons learned often to clients to remind them to ask themselves, "What is the most important thing I want to achieve? And what do I need to stop, continue, or more of to reach this achievement?"

Heard's story about the hospital raises a vitally important point. The core idea here isn't to be the best. It's to be the best at what matters most. Sometimes there's a critically important difference between those two ideas. One thing's for sure, you will never achieve the position of being the best unless you take care of what matters most.

For Alabama Football, It's Process

Look at the approach that many successful sports coaches take. A prime example is Coach Nick Saban of the University of Alabama football team. At the time of this writing, Alabama is the reigning national football champion and is on track to do it again this year.

Coach Saban, like many other great coaches, says that the key to being the best is to keep your head down and focus on process. If you are the best at what matters most right in front of you—whether it's in the weight room or on the practice field—and you carry that focus on process into the game and execute well, then you will succeed.

Staying with the example of a hospital, we can learn lessons from health care about how the world is changing for every business and how that's affecting our area of focus. Today, more than ever, you have to incorporate what matters most to the customer into what they do. It's happening in businesses where it's never happened before, including health care.

Treating Patients Like Customers

A few years ago the *New York Times* published an article about the then-new idea in health care of treating patients more like customers. A doctor wrote a letter to the editor in which he ranted and raved about how the very last thing we needed in health care was to treat patients like customers. In his mind, it demeaned and cheapened the whole concept of health care. He said that he would never treat patients like customers and that the very thought of doing so was anathema to him. (Author's note: This is the first time I've ever had the opportunity to use the word *anathema* in a book. It feels great.)

Upon reading his letter, I wrote my own letter to the editor in which I said that, as an occasional patient and buyer of health care services, I would absolutely welcome a health care system, including all doctors and hospitals, that would treat me with anywhere near the kind of great personal service I received from a Ritz Carlton or even a Starbucks. My problem with many doctors and hospitals has been that they make it all about them, rather than all about the patients and their families.

On a personal note, let me say that I am currently fortunate in having a doctor who places what matters most to me at the top of her focus list. She is incredibly focused not only on her patients' physical well-being but on their concerns and feelings as well.

I have no idea what lapse in judgment caused the *New York Times* to decide not to publish my letter. Upon reflection, perhaps it ran a bit too long. I tend to rant when I get excited about something.

When Patients Talk Back

Fast-forward to the present day. Oh my, how things have changed. I invite you to visit http://hospitalcompare.hhs .gov/. This is the U.S. Department of Health and Human Services' Medicare Hospital Compare Quality of Care Compare Page. What's happening is that patient satisfaction ratings are now a factor in how much money a hospital gets paid by Medicare. What we're talking about here is customer satisfaction.

Visit the website and enter the name of your city into the form. You'll see a list of all the hospitals in your area. Choose three of them to compare, and you will then be taken to a series of pages that show patient satisfaction ratings with such things as how well the nurses communicated with the patient, how well the doctors communicated with the patient, how well the patient's pain was controlled, the degree to which hospital staff explained the medicines, whether or not the patient's room and bathroom were always clean, whether the area around the patient's room was always quiet at night, and much, much more.

Patients also rate the hospitals regarding their level of care for different medical conditions, such as heart attacks, pneumonia, surgical care, children's asthma, and more.

The site also shows the percentage of patients rating each hospital overall as 9 or 10 (on a 10-point scale). In my hometown of Nashville, the top three rated hospitals at the time I checked the website were the Hospital for Spinal Surgery, Saint Thomas Hospital, and Centennial Medical Center. It was a complete list that went all the way to the hospital ranked rock bottom, where I hope I never end up if I am in need of medical care.

The Patients' Lists

This new sensitivity to patients and how their ratings will affect payment by Medicare is causing hospitals to do things such as reduce noise levels at night on patient floors, keep the place cleaner, and do a better job of communicating with patients. They've realized that what matters most includes what's on the patients' lists and not just the doctor's list.

For the first time, hospitals aren't getting to make up the rules about what matters most. Of course, everyone, including the doctors, the hospitals, and the patients, put the actual medical care at the top of the list. Now, the patients, as customers, are having a say in what else goes on the list. We are going to see these customer ratings begin to play a big part in the marketing programs of hospitals. Those with high ratings will tell the world. Those with low ratings will have to do what they need to do to catch up.

What it means to you and your business is simple. Most of your customers are, have been, or will be patients in hospitals. They will now have a chance to rate those hospitals and to make future choices based on those ratings being made public. They will be empowered as customers, and that empowerment will affect decisions they make about everyone they do business with, including you.

Once people have fired a hospital or two, they won't think twice about firing you or me if we don't measure up on what matters most to them. Don't be distracted by being best at what's ultimately unimportant. Make it simple. Focus. Take action.

Questions to Consider

- What are three ways that you can immediately improve your performance on the basics?
- What do you do well that you take for granted?
- Where have you said "good enough" and stopped improving?
- What do your customers care about that you don't give enough thought or attention to?
- How will you find out what those things are?
- What customers will you invite to help you improve what you do?
- When will you contact them?

14

Clarity, Process, and Profit
bytes of knowledge

How They Did It

"Joe, give me a very specific, real-world example of a company that has used the idea of being the best at what matters most to improve its business and increase profit. Tell me how it did it."

Okay. Here you go.

In 2005, in my book *Indispensable: How to Become the Company Your Customers Can't Live Without,* here's what I wrote about a company called bytes of knowledge:

> My computers go down or develop a mystery mal-function and I go into default mode. I call bytes of knowledge, someone comes over and fixes the problem, then they send me a bill and I pay it. I know for a fact that others charge less. This is irrelevant to me. I am typical of today's customer who places a high value on depend-ability and consistency of performance. I'm looking for the sure thing. I don't have the time, patience, or money to waste on any company that can't get it right the first time

Things have changed pretty dramatically for bytes of knowledge since 2005. The company has grown into a full-service provider of technology solutions for small to mid-size businesses, entrepreneurs, start-ups, and corporate, nonprofit, and government clients. Its areas of expertise include the design and development of software pro-ducts, mobile apps, websites, interactive training, strategic consulting, network infrastructure, and much more. The company has 21 employees and revenue approaching $3 million.

The First Order of Business

Julie and Charles May are the founding principals of bytes of knowledge (hereafter referred to as b:ok), with Julie serving as chief executive officer (CEO). Julie says that the core values at b:ok dictate that they make technology easy for their clients. Their brand promise is hassle-free technology. They've always had clarity on that.

At bytes of knowledge the first order of business is to determine what matters most to their customers. Julie says, "Successful projects begin with a shared vision, are developed through open communication, and are delivered without surprises. Now, anybody can say that, but the fact of the matter is that technology folks generally don't have the business background and facilitation experience to uncover the critical business needs and align the appropriate technology."

The key is in listening with focus and intent to the client's perspective. It's about the client's agenda, not b:ok's.

"We are platform agnostic, so we don't just apply the tools we know," Julie says. "We ask our clients about the strategic goals of their investment in technology and then we listen. Then we ask them the questions that most of them, frankly, don't know to ask, and they are grateful we do. If we have a client who comes to us with a technical solution in mind, we will fully vet it to see if it does make sense for ROI [return on investment] and the predetermined technology. Often the technology and the ROI are not complementary, so we suggest reshaping the project to make sure these are in full alignment."

What matters most to clients is results, so everyone at b:ok puts a great focus on the planning and process aspects of client relations. "We get a lot of rescue projects, the ones that did not get done right the first time," Julie says. "There are a variety of reasons for this, but frankly many projects go awry because the planning and processes were not there from the start and were not based on business objectives that were aligned with technical strategy. Why? Because the technicians don't always use the best processes to begin with, so how can they help you with yours?"

They Are a Business Partner

Here's an absolute key to success that b:ok has discovered. It isn't just a vendor but a business partner. The staff don't just understand technology and their side of the business. At b:ok, employees are trained to understand key business functions, such as sales, human resources, operations, marketing, and accounting and consider these workflows into the technical solution. This is a huge differentiator from many of b:ok's competitors who are great at understanding their particular technology solutions but not so great at understanding the fundamentals of their clients' businesses.

b:ok has found a way to do what matters most both for the client and for its own business—and at the same time, it teaches all employees how businesses work. This makes them more valuable partners to clients and at the same time keeps everyone focused on the internal goal: profit.

They Could Be Doing Better

A few years ago, b:ok was doing well and growing steadily, but Julie and Charles believed that they could be doing better with the great people and resources that they had. In thinking through what matters most, they kept coming back to profit as the key metric that could be used to galvanize the entire team, create a unified focus, and drive much better results.

Julie and Charles knew that any process they used to focus on improving profit would have to be built on a foundation of culture. One employee had said, "People don't know who we are." This was a wake-up call to get serious and intentional about defining a culture that would support the growth of the company and the careers of everyone there.

Defining Their Culture

The entire company "sat around and came up with it." For b: ok, defining culture was a matter of declaring, "We are communication experts," and declaring that they saw them-selves as "creative, accountable, empowering, trustworthy, and responsive." They then listed the core beliefs of values, qualities, and ethics that would be the guidelines for behavior both internally and externally.

The values: employee "uberfaction," customer delight, innovation, and sustainability
The qualities: leadership, reliability, relationship focus, and
  pizzazz
The ethics: honesty, integrity, respect, and teamwork

If you are wondering whether or not this is the way you should develop your own culture, I go back to my standard answer: Yes, if it works for you. Remember that culture development, identification of values, determining what mat-ters most, or any other process has to be personal to you and your team. What works for 3M won't work for Disney, and what works for Disney won't work for the Pancake Pantry. Have the courage to say, "This is what feels right to us," then go for it.

One key reason why a focus on profit worked for b:ok was that everyone understood that the value of sustainability wasn't just environmental; it also meant financial sustainability. This fundamental understanding of the business of running a business in a viable way was vital to the success of the process they employed.

The Monday Morning Boost

To reinforce the importance of b:ok's culture as something very real that employees use to guide behavior every day, they use what they call the Monday Morning Boost. Every employee at the Monday morning meeting has a small paper form that, on one side, lets them give "kudos" to another member of the team. They record "here's what they did" to deserve the shout-out, and on the flip side of the form, they circle the aspects of the culture, all of which are listed, that the team member's actions exemplified.

This kind of low-tech, simple, very personal reinforcement of a company's values and culture is what makes it worth more than the paper or computer it's written on. Too often, people decide that "it's time we came up with" a culture, or a vision statement, or a mission statement, or whatever other thing they have heard that a company is supposed to have. Then they hire a consultant or facilitator, do a weekend off-site gathering at a state park or resort, fill the walls with sheets of paper covered with ideas, put it all together, print it up, frame it and hang it in the break room, declare victory, and forget about it until the next meeting, when they all pull their wallet-size versions out of their pockets to read in unison. Then they forget about it again.

Why even bother? If you're not going to make your culture real and constantly reinforce it in terms of how everyone thinks and acts with one another, customers, and the rest of the world, what's the point? Charles and Julie are determined to make culture a foundation from which great things can be built.

The next step is to create a process that creates success around what matters most. Because the concept of process is so important to the sustainability of any business, let's define it. *Process* is a series of steps or actions taken to achieve an end. It is a collection of related, structured activities or tasks that serve a particular goal. It begins with a mission objective and continues to sustain and improve on the continuing achievement of the objective. Process is how you create success. It's how you get there when you're trying to move up. Process is how you stay there once you succeed. It's totally different than a project. Process never ends.

Plug the Holes in the Bucket

Charles and Julie looked at the profit picture at b:ok and determined that for the level of business they were doing, the bottom line results simply weren't good enough and they weren't realizing the profitability they wanted. They could see weaknesses in the system, such as employees not entering time properly, losing invoicing opportunities, and more. Julie said that they had to "plug the holes in the bucket."

Driven by the objective of what mattered most, to increase profitability, Julie developed "The Five Cs," which was a simple way of looking at workflow from revenue opportunity to invoicing. The Five Cs are:

1. *Contact:* Enter the prospect's contact information, identify the sales resource team, enter the opportunity with dollar value, schedule research, schedule appointments, create and revise the proposal, create a contract, follow up with the prospect, close the opportunity—won/lost/no decision.
2. *Contract:* Have the contract signed, create the work plan, determine the project resource team, make service requests, schedule appointments, follow up.
3. *Communicate:* Review/revise the work plan, coordinate with the client, all service or project communication, enter opportunity with dollar amount on change order or new business, enter the time and document against activity, check hours against the work plan, enter the time and invoice.
4. *Check-in:* Update the work plans and templates with improvements, survey the client, conduct quarterly reviews, set a time to reinitiate contact.
5. *Contact:* Continue the process by setting dates and times to talk with the client about new opportunities that were exposed during the 5 Cs process.

The Five Cs plan took the idea of what mattered most at b:ok, from the idea stage to the action stage. It's relatively easy to come up with an idea of what matters most, whether it's improving profitability, making the world a better place, satisfying customers, ensuring consistency, or any other objective. It's much tougher to take the next step and determine what activities will actually drive the achievement of what matters most.

Workflow and Time Tracking

At b:ok, Julie and Charles didn't stop with the 5C's, Julie thought there were still too many opportunities for holes in the bucket and "things that could easily have been prevented." They needed a way to actually track and manage every hour spent by every employee to ensure that the entire team maintained focus on what mattered most.

Julie and Charles elected to use a workflow and time tracking system provided by ConnectWise, a business automation solutions company specializing in helping information technology (IT) clients. The point here is not that you have to use an outside solution to manage your workflow or anything else, although there are great resources available to help just about any company manage its business better. The point is that without some sort of system or discipline to manage work and the ability to create and report on metrics, it's difficult to stay on point with what matters most. Julie says, "Sometimes it all boils down to math."

Get a Checklist

Let me jump in here with an endorsement of the book *The Checklist Manifesto,* by Atul Gawande. The idea in Gawande's book is simple and profound. He makes the case that we must organize what we do in a way that empowers people to do their best work, communicate effectively at crucial points, and do a much better job of getting things done. Gawande, a surgeon, explains that for a range of endeavors and professions, from pilots to doctors to engineers who build skyscrapers, the answer is to have a checklist.

What Julie and Charles do at b:ok is a pretty sophisticated and high-tech version of a checklist, a system that keeps us on track. Being the best at what matters most means that we create alignment between our objectives and our activities. It means that we must work with intention, not just reacting to what comes up during the day but proactively managing our activities according to predetermined priorities. It can be done with a sophisticated solution or with something as simple as a to-do list on a piece of paper. But it must be done.

Everything Tracked through the System

At b:ok, the perfect solution was ConnectWise. It's a metrics program in which every employee enters all of their time and activities. b:ok has had it for six years, and Julie and Charles say it took them about two years to really get it "under our belts" and begin to fully realize the benefits. Now it's how b:ok manages and tracks everything.

Every Friday, b:ok has a Steering Committee meeting of the b:ok leadership team. At this meeting they use the information from ConnectWise to help make decisions about virtually everything in the business. The Five Cs are all tracked through the system. They have classified every activity into "work types," including training, accounting, sales ambassador, customer service, internal communication, regular (revenue-generating activities), nonprofit/community service, operations management, marketing, and more.

The work activities are color-coded. Red is work they don't get paid for, yellow is what they do to create business, and green is what they do to earn money (billable activity). When an employee records work activity, he or she codes it with a work type and a work role. Absolutely every activity is on the time sheets, including what's billable and what's not. Julie says that "every single minute is accountable."

Educating the Employees and Getting Buy-In

I asked about employee resistance to such a system. These are mostly young employees, and I wondered how they reacted to having to account for every minute and to being so intensely observed.

Julie and Charles believe that the average employee at most companies really isn't given the opportunity to learn what makes a company run. So at b:ok they take the time to educate everyone about how the company works, how it makes money, and thus how everyone gets paid. They share numbers such as revenue against costs, costs per quarter, and basically just where all the money goes once it comes in.

Here's a key to buy-in from the employees: b:ok funds a pool of money that is 33 percent of the amount of revenue beyond the company's projected sustainability goal. If they reach beyond sustainability to what they call their "stretch goal," the fund is 50 percent of the revenue beyond that. The employees share in that revenue. It resets every quarter.

This process has fundamentally changed the focus of everyone in the company and the way people do their work. Everyone understands that putting in your time properly on the time sheet is what b:ok needs to properly fund the profit-sharing program. Having this big-picture understanding of the business has motivated employees to bring b:ok ways to save money, which impacts profitability as much as revenue.

How to Run a Business

Charles and Julie believe that they are now teaching people how to run a business. Employees understand the dollars and cents for their own business, which gives them a better understanding of it for the clients' businesses, which makes them a more valuable resource.

At b:ok, because they embraced the idea of being the best at what matters most, they have identified "what should be" in terms of how time should be spent and can now compare that to what is. Then they can talk about it and make adjustments. The overarching principle is knowing what's important, how we spend our time, and how we are doing in terms of being the best at what's important.

The Coffee Shop Generation

As for being so intensely observed, Charles points out that the employees feel that if you're doing a good job, you're happy to be watched. What the system does is give people ongoing, very current, very relevant feedback, which every employee wants. People want to know how they are doing. The other factor is that so many of the employees are young, what Julie refers to as "the coffee shop generation." Julie says, "This is the generation who goes to the coffee shop and their laptops are literally in their laps. They love to work without walls, they love the noise, and they want unique experiences just for them. Most of all they want to collaborate."

Julie and Charles understand the generation that works for them: they love the financial transparency through sharing and understanding of all of the company's numbers. It engenders confidence that the business is working properly. It also engenders a feeling of "we're all in this together." Charles says, "Anyone can say 'Hey, I was thinking . . .' There's no such thing as a bad idea."

This is a good story. But does this stuff really work? b:ok's 2012 profitability increased 425 percent over the previous year. Julie and Charles attribute this largely to having a process that lets everyone in the organization be the best at what matters most to both the client and the company all the time.

Questions to Consider

- Do you have clarity on your core values as they relate to your brand?
- Do the marketplace and your customers have clarity on your brand?
- Do you follow your agenda or your customer's agenda?
- Can you see the world through your customers' perspectives?
- Do you and your team truly understand your customers?
- If you are in the business-to-business arena, do you know more about your customers and prospects than any of your competitors could possibly know?
- On a scale of 1 to 10, how would you rank your company in terms of everyone truly understanding and believing in your values, qualities, and ethics?
- List all the ways in which you regularly make your culture real.
- How do you track your activities as related to what matters most?

- Do your employees or colleagues understand what makes your company run?
- Do your employees know how they are doing?
- Do they get ongoing, current, relevant feedback?
- Do you understand what motivates your employees?
- Does everyone in your business share a feeling of "we're all in this together"?
- If not, how can you begin to engender that feeling?

15

What Matters Most to Your Team

Understanding Employees Matters, Too

To be the best at what matters most, it's essential to get buy-in from your team. It's therefore essential to know what matters most to the people on your team. It's one thing for you to want your team to have the same goals and objectives that you have. It's quite another to assume that they're motivated to reach those goals the same way you are.

Just like we have to understand our customers and what matters most to them, we have to understand our employees and coworkers and what matters most to them, too. In these days of multiple generations working together under one company roof, it's easy to fall into the trap of thinking that "they" are wrong in what they want, how they want it, and why they want it.

They're usually not wrong about those things any more than you are; they're just different. Most of us have business relationships with people who live completely different lifestyles than we do. What's it worth to me and the strength and effectiveness of my relationships if those other people feel that I "get them." It's worth quite a bit.

Understanding

One great strength that Julie and Charles May bring to the success of their company, bytes of knowledge, is an understanding of their young employees and what matters to them. Julie wrote a blog on this that I think is worth sharing.

"We Are the Coffee Shop Generation," by Julie May

We want everything flexible. From what we wear, to how we interact, to the way we work, to when we work, to where we work. We want our experience custom-ized, even down to our coffee. We are the coffee shop generation.

We want to wear jeans to work. We want to wear cool imprinted t-shirts everyday. Flip-flops are preferred, all year round, of course. We probably have at least one tattoo and, likely a piercing. We wear vintage clothes because we believe in sustainability. We eat natural and organic foods, with an occasional Egg McMuffin thrown in the mix. We need windows and fresh air. We need our freedom, otherwise we will rebel or get anxious. We are the coffee shop generation.

We don't want to be limited. We prefer a much less formal communication style. We put ourselves out "there." We tell our life story through social media channels. We are connected and yet dispersed. We are complex yet transparent. We want to make a differ-ence in our community and impact all mankind. We like to work and play with our peers. We are the coffee shop generation.

We want to collaborate and work in teams. We are global thinkers. Our heads and our information are in the clouds, but not the cloud you used to know. We need our earbuds to focus when we work and listen to our personalized music stream. We need the ambient noise to energize us. We are the coffee shop generation.

We are gypsies. Desktops are archaic. We are mobile, we work where we want. We don't want walls or cubicles, we want to put our feet up with our computers in our laps. That's why they are called laptops, anyway, right? We consider wireless access as a primary utility like water and electricity.

We want the coffee we want (dammit), and we are very specific about what it is and how it is prepared. What, you mean you can't do that? We want options so we can make choices that are unique to us as individuals. If you don't have the answer, we will Google it. Who needs the speculation anyway? If we have ADD we may even brag about it because it means we can multi-task better. If we are having trouble we just drink more coffee, the way we want it . . . and lots of it. Yes, that's our cure. We are the coffee shop generation.

Questions to Consider

- How well do you know your employees, colleagues, and customers in terms of what matters in their lives?
- How can you learn more about them?
- Do you expect everyone around you to be motivated by the same things and in the same ways as you are?
- If so, how's that working out for you?

16

Culture Drives Results

That's a Shame

Culture is a word that often gets an eye roll from business leaders. It sounds like one of those squishy ideas that busy, important captains of industry don't have time to think about or deal with because they're so busy creating results.

That's a shame. Actually it's more than a shame. It's a failure of leadership, because your culture drives your results— or your lack of them.

Your organization already has a culture. It's not something that you come up with on a leadership retreat. It's how everyone in your organization behaves with one another and everyone else, including partners, vendors, prospects, customers, the people on the elevator, the person on the phone, the person who sent the e-mail, the upset customer who comments on your Facebook page, or anyone out there who you have any contact with in any way.

By Accident or Intentional?

You can't not have a culture. The only question is whether your organization's culture was created by accident or created with intention. If you are going to be the best at what matters most, you have to be very intentional about culture.

Your culture is the real-life, everyday version of your values being played out among your people. Your culture is what matters most to you internally, as a team. By the way, if you are a one-person business, you have a culture just as much as Apple or BMW has a culture.

Everything in Alignment

In terms of culture, the goal is to get everything that matters most in alignment. That means that your stated values are, in fact, the same as the values that are actually experienced in the hallways, on the phone, in e-mails, or with any other form of human contact. Alignment means that what happens when the boss is gone or when no one is looking is the same as what happens when the boss is sitting in the room. Alignment means that what matters most internally lines up perfectly with what matters most to the customer.

If your culture isn't in alignment, you will fail to reach your potential. When culture isn't in alignment, your performance is automatically being held back. If you ever lie awake at night worrying about why your company isn't performing as well as you feel it should be, then the chances are very good that you've got a culture that's out of alignment.

Here's a good metaphor for culture alignment. Imagine 25 geese flying around in all different directions, willy-nilly, bumping into one another up there in the sky. That's an organization out of alignment. Now imagine those same 25 geese all moving into the classic V formation, everyone focused and heading in the same direction, moving as a team in total support of one another. That's alignment.

Making Culture Mean Something

I recently worked with a wonderful company in the Midwest that has about 50 employees. The chief executive officer (CEO) went through the process of having all employees contribute to forming a list of values that they would hold as a guideline for how they worked as a company. This would be their culture. This would be what mattered most.

They ended up with values that included fun, mutual respect, caring for the community, always honoring the customer, and a handful of other mutually agreed-upon attributes or factors. The agreement was that this is how they choose to play, and no one was exempt from these rules of the road.

I participated in the daylong employee event where their list of values was to be officially unveiled to everyone in the company. On the day of the event I found out that the week before, the CEO had "fired" their biggest client. Although it meant a loss in revenue, it meant a gain in the confidence and respect of every single employee. The fact was that this client simply played by a different set of rules that was in conflict with the company's values. There was no way to be in alignment from a culture or values standpoint with this client. What matters most sometimes means knowing what business to walk away from, no matter what the short-term cost in dollars.

The other action taken the week before the values rollout meeting was that the CEO fired a member of the senior leadership team. This executive had been presented with the values and he said that he wasn't going to change his way of working with others, which unfortunately included a lack of respect, simply to adhere to what he referred to as a "silly list of kindergarten playground rules." The CEO fired him.

The result was, much as with the firing of the client, a boost in morale for the whole company, as the CEO had demonstrated that these values truly are what matters most, and we're not kidding around about it. We've decided what matters most, and if you disagree, that's fine, but you can't work here. That's what leadership looks like.

You Have to Fire Them

I take a fairly ruthless stand about what you do with people in the organization who violate the clearly stated and agreed-upon values of the organization. Every truly effective leader I've ever worked with feels the same way. If, for example, your values state that you treat everyone with respect, and you've got a top performer who is disrespectful of others, then you invite him or her to change, and if the person doesn't, you fire him or her.

I also think that it has to be, in a way, a public execution. By that I mean that you do what the CEO did who fired the member of the senior leadership team. There was no announcement that said, "He left to pursue other opportunities." The CEO told the team that the fired executive had been openly disrespectful of employees and that it was behavior that would not be tolerated. Period.

Culture is about what's accepted and not accepted. Culture is what's approved of and disapproved of. To the extent that you tolerate people in the organization who violate the standards of the culture, you lose the confidence of every other employee. You can't say, "This matters most," and then turn a blind eye to those who violate that standard.

Your culture is what matters most in the sense that it's like drawing boundaries, and no one can go outside those boundaries. "No one" includes a performance superstar. It means that if your greatest revenue producer violates the values of the culture, he or she has to go. If the employee stays, leadership becomes a joke. No one will believe in the organization, and no one will get behind the goals of the company.

Truly great organizations and even individual performers adhere to a culture that is crystal clear, and that eventually becomes part of the DNA. Your culture, your values, your sense of what matters most become what determines the behaviors that won't be tolerated by anyone, including co-workers. There are certain things that just aren't done, and there are other things that are always the way it's done. Upholding the values of the culture with consistency is one of the greatest responsibilities and obligations of leadership.

Who Would Stay? Who Would Go?

My friend Elizabeth Crook is the founder and CEO of Orchard Advisors (orchardadvisors.com). She suggests this wonderfully simple and effective way to determine the values that are already what matters most to you. If you were to start your business over again and you could choose whomever you wanted from the existing organization to go with you, whom would you choose? Think about how the ones you would choose behave and how they conduct their business. They embody the behaviors that you value.

Now think about the ones you know you'd leave behind. Some of them may not make the chosen list purely because of performance issues. They may simply lack the skills or ability to do the work. But some of them will likely not make your list because of their particular set of values. The way they behave and work with others is unacceptable to you.

So now you're left with quite a challenge. If you do have conflicting values within the organization, then you are most definitely not in alignment. If you are not in alignment, then you are performing at a level far below where you could and should be.

This inevitably leads to a very, very challenging question: Who needs to be here, and who needs to go? If not that, then certainly a frank discussion of what our values are, what matters most here, and how we go about getting everyone on that same page.

In your process of determining what matters most and who's on board with it, I am a great believer in keeping it as simple as possible. Choose three or four values that resonate with everyone. It's easy to get carried away and end up with a list of two dozen, but that ends up being virtually meaningless. Determining what matters most internally in terms of values and culture should be a gut-level thing as much as or more than an intellectual thing. Once it's defined and agreed upon, it should be enforced and reinforced constantly, forever and ever, without end.

True North

What matters most should make you smile. It should give you guidance. It should serve to help make the most of your big decisions in advance. It should be a compass that points true North.

Questions to Consider

- In your business, what behaviors are absolutely expected from everyone and by everyone? What behaviors are not acceptable?
- Does anyone in your organization consistently violate those rules of acceptable behavior?
- Why is this person still there?

- What behaviors are unacceptable from clients or customers?
- Are there any customers that you need to fire?
- How do you regularly reinforce your culture with your team?
- How would people who do business with you describe you/your company? What words would 90 percent of them use?
- What do you need to change?
- What do you need to do now?

17

How Brands Win

Consistently Better at the Basics

Let's look at some of the Top 10 Most Trusted Brands as determined in a survey by *Entrepreneur* magazine and the Values Institute. Did these brands win with exotic marketing and wow factor? Or did they win by being the best at what matters most? Is their advantage that they are distinctly unique through being different? Or are they different because they are consistently better at the basics?

Amazon

Amazon wins with low prices, free shipping on orders over a minimum total, free shipping and streaming movies to Prime members, an endless selection of almost any product you can think of, knowledge of customers through their past purchases (which enables Amazon to recommend products that they like), quick-shipping options, one-click purchasing, and ease of doing business.

It's that last one, being easy to do business with, that's won me over as a loyal customer. A few months ago, a lightbulb went out in a kitchen undercounter light fixture in our home. It was a tiny, unusual lightbulb, and I anticipated difficulty in finding a replacement. I managed to track down the manufacturer of the bulb and did what I often do when I'm looking to buy any product, especially one that I am unfamiliar with or don't know where I can buy it. I went to Amazon.com.

I put the manufacturer's name and the model number of the lightbulb into the Amazon search engine, and voilà, there it was. Not only did Amazon make this hard-to-find item easy to find, I was able to purchase it with the one click and the shipping was free. Amazon won the "easy to do business with" prize that day, and once again, the company locked me in as a loyal customer.

Coca-Cola

Coca-Cola wins by being everywhere, thus easy to do business with, and through consistency of product. By the way, Coca-Cola was the only company that didn't receive a single negative mark in the Top 10 Most Trusted Brands survey.

So let's think about this. Coca-Cola is always the same. There are no surprises. What might that have to do with your company?

I recently worked with one of the top home-building companies in the country. One of their basic rules of business is a "no surprises" policy. In my own business I find that the foundation of our reputation is that we are completely boring in terms of always delivering quality. We don't believe in surprises. We believe in quality every single time.

If you look at the performance of every company on this list, and every company that you love to do business with, large or small, one of their attributes is that you can depend on them. They deliver quality every single time. I have long said that consistency of performance is the great brand builder. Inconsistency of performance is the ultimate brand killer.

FedEx

FedEx wins with consistency of performance and personal connections with customers. Not surprisingly, the company received its strongest ratings in ability, specifically for being able to achieve what it promises and for the efficiency of its operations.

I do business with both FedEx and UPS. They are worthy competitors and serve to keep each other in a state of constant improvement. The key competitive issue is simple: Do you deliver my package on time? If either FedEx or UPS starts to lose there, then it's game over.

I like our UPS and FedEx delivery guys and gals. They are always courteous and friendly and are a pleasure to do business with. Smiling faces wouldn't make up for late deliveries, though. Get the basics right, or you don't get to play.

Apple

Aha! Now here's the one with the wow factor! The exotic, mysterious, edgy silver bullets! Right? Nope. Apple is innovative right smack in the middle of what customers value most, from products that are so easy to use that they don't need instruction manuals to retail stores that are easy to do business with. Apple innovates inside the box on what matters most to their customers.

To me, Apple is one of the best examples of a company that is so good at the basics that it is cutting edge. Apple also leads the way in having products that are easy to use. Apple devices are so simple that you can operate them almost intuitively.

Target

Survey respondents said that what they love about Target is clean stores, competitive pricing, attractive merchandise, trendy clothing at great prices, friendly employees, and enough employees in the store to serve customers well.

This is getting monotonous, isn't it? Winning on the basics. Let's do a few more.

Ford

Ford wins with a refocus on what matters most, including stability, dependability, and "behaving responsibly" (as worded by survey respondents).

Starbucks

Starbucks wins with espresso-based coffee that you either love or don't, and its target market loves it. Starbucks also wins with incredible selection and an environment that invites people to stay.

Southwest Airlines

Put aside all of the wonderful stories about quirky and entertaining flight attendants. People tell those stories all the time as if they are the reason for the consistent success of Southwest Airlines in what is arguably the toughest industry in the world.

Let me assure you, the singing flight attendants are the cherry on top of the cake. It's not why Southwest wins. The cake is why Southwest wins. The cake is that Southwest Airlines is an extremely proficient operation that gets people and their luggage from point A to point B in a low-cost, efficient manner, and it does so better than anyone else.

I was working with an insurance group and a woman told a great story about a trip that she made on Southwest Airlines with one of her friends. It was her friend's birthday, and the woman told one of the flight attendants. About halfway through the flight, the flight attendant announced to everyone that there was a special birthday gal on board. He dimmed the cabin lights, had everyone turn on their flight attendant call button to be the "candles," gave out extra peanuts as party goodies, and the entire plane sang "Happy Birthday" to the woman's friend.

After she finished the story, I asked her why she had flown Southwest Airlines in the first place. She said, "Because they had the lowest fare, bags fly free, and they are almost always on time." When you win on the basics, you win.

Nordstrom

Nordstrom wins with a culture of customer service. It is famous for going above and beyond for customers. It has a very liberal return policy, often sends thank-you notes, and through actions like these, has won undying loyalty from legions of customers.

Nordstrom doesn't have the lowest price, but its culture of really great customer attention and service earns Nordstrom the right to charge more. Nordstrom is a prime example of how a superior value proposition can win a market niche even when competitors offer lower prices on exactly the same products.

It Works

The message from these winners in the Most Trusted Brand survey is unmistakable. Each of them wins in meeting their customers' high expectations on dependability, customer service, competitive pricing, and being easy to do business with. Thus they establish and sustain their positions as market leaders.

Focus on what matters the most. It works.

Questions to Consider

- On a scale of 1 to 10, how easy are you to do business with?
- What are the three areas you need to improve to be easier to do business with?
- Do your customers have to think too much to do business with you?
- Do you make your value proposition so clear that they immediately get it?
- Do you have to explain what you do and the value of it more than you should have to?
- How can you make doing business with you simpler for your customers?
- Does the value your company offers make you the logical first choice for customers?
- If you are not the lowest-priced choice, do you do a good-enough job of explaining total value?
- Think about each of these great brands. What does each one do well that you emulate?
  - Amazon
  - Coca-Cola
  - FedEx
  - Apple
  - Target
  - Ford
  - Starbucks
  - Southwest Airlines
  - Nordstrom

18

How the Internet Is Killing Hype

Why You Bought the Chutney

A Cisco Systems advertisement said it perfectly:

> Old Days: You bought the chutney because you liked the jar.

> New Days: You bought the chutney because everyone likes the chutney.

Some would say that we are in the age of flash and attention getting, and that it's all about the "jar," meaning the shiny package of marketing that we wrap around our business to attract customers. In fact, the exact opposite is true. The days of winning in the market through your ability to glitz up your business through wildly imaginative marketing and promotion are gone. Forever.

The Internet is killing hype.

If you buy chutney today because you loved the look of the jar it was in and upon tasting that chutney you really don't like it, your next stop is the Internet. You go online and tell the world that the chutney stinks. As more people taste the stinky chutney in the fabulous jar, they also go online and tell the world.

It doesn't take long before the chutney company is out of business. In the old days, word-of-mouth, reviews took quite a while to get around. You told your neighbor that the movie you saw was terrible, that the hotel your family stayed in during vacation had mold in the room, or that the chutney you bought was stinky.

Now it takes you less than a minute online to tell hundreds of people. They repost your comments to reach thousands. Then those thousands spread the word to reach the rest of the world.

Hype is dead. Long live quality. If you don't deliver the goods in today's world, you're busted.

Consumers Aren't Shy

The ability of today's customers, and that includes business-to-business buyers, to instantly communicate their dissatisfaction with product or service quality to the world has doomed substandard performance.

"Consumers are demanding better service more now than ever before, and they're not shy about voicing their displeasure after getting bad service," says Angie's List founder Angie Hicks. "The good news for companies that provide great customer service is that consumers are sharing those experiences as well. That kind of positive word-of-mouth marketing is invaluable to most business owners."

It's not just about retail customers either. Today's business-to-business customer goes straight to the Internet to get feedback on every business-to-business service and product imaginable. Beyond online platforms, they also utilize user conferences, product seminars, and other live events to exchange information on satisfaction and dissatisfaction with their business-to-business transactions and relationships.

They're Talking about You

Your customers are talking about you right now behind your back. Customer comments like these flood the Internet through websites such as Yelp.com, Facebook, TripAdvisor .com, and blogs, blogs, and more blogs:

> Nice try! Your ads are catchy but your service is just average.

> I should have listened to my friends who said "don't shop there!" but I fell for the hype. Other stores have a better selection and more helpful employees.

> Their website promised great consulting services but all they did was give us a report on what we already knew. What a colossal waste of money.

> They said that they "wow" their customers, and they did it with me. Wow—the extras they give you don't make up for the mediocre products, mediocre service, and employees who clearly wish they were somewhere else. Wow—you should get better at the basics.

The real problem is that all of these businesses that were slammed in customer reviews probably believe that they're doing just fine on the basics. It's the great illusion that we're all beyond the idea of winning business through consistent quality. We're looking for the wow factor.

And so, instead of being so innovative and so amazing at the basics that we are cutting edge, we focus on the extras, and in doing so, we neglect the basics.

Palm Trees, Azure Blue Skies, and . . . Cockroaches

I was looking for a hotel on a beach where I could go and do some work on this book. One hotel in particular seemed like a good possibility. I checked out the hotel's website, then immediately went to a travel review site (that I almost always go to) to see what hotel customers had to say about their experiences there. There was a bit of a contrast between what the hotel website had to say and what a big percentage of the customers who reviewed the hotel had to say:

Hotel website: "A fabulous destination for family fun."
Traveler review: "Just a nightmare for a family with small children."

Hotel website: "Immaculately landscaped garden grounds which offer incredible views."
Traveler review: "Blech. The room smelled like mold and mildew."

Hotel website: "Unwind to the sounds of the sea."
Traveler review: "A room that clearly smelled like mold."

Hotel website: "A delightful day enjoying the beautiful sunshine, sights, and sounds."
Traveler review: "Horrible. Do not bother."

Hotel website: "Plush beds with cotton linens and soft pillows."
Traveler review: "There are large stains on the bedroom walls and ceilings."

Hotel website: "The guest room areas, most with beautiful views and expansive balconies, provide a great place to sit back, smell the ocean breeze and soak up the beauty of the lush hotel's surroundings."
Traveler review: "Nasty. Smelled like mold and mildew."

Hotel website: "Palm trees, azure blue skies, and plenty of sunshine."

Traveler review: "Cockroaches!"

"I Would Like to Apologize"

Regular users of travel customer review sites learn to spot the bogus reviews from angry people who give every hotel they visit a bad review. There are also bad reviews posted by competitors or people who had one thing go wrong and exaggerate their negative experience.

But the terrible reviews of this particular hotel were many in number and a very high percentage of total reviews, and they were often accompanied by photos of whatever they were complaining about. Many were posted by frequent reviewers who had given very good reviews to other hotels. These weren't habitual complainers.

Furthermore, the hotel manager had responded to almost every negative review with statements that invariably began with "I would like to apologize for . . . " Even he wasn't contesting the validity of the complaints. In each of his responses, he said that he had passed along the complaint to the hotel staff and that they would all do better in the future. I've always said that managers who spend an inordinate amount of time apologizing are simply really bad managers. I don't want apologies. I want the manager to train the staff to do it right.

Do What You Say You'll Do

So when it's a business website versus customers, who wins? It's not a fair fight. Today, customers can tear down a company's reputation in the blink of an eye. This is how the Internet is killing hype. If you are not providing good value at what matters most to customers, you will not be long for the marketplace. You have to keep the promises that you make. You have to do what we say you'll do. Your customers talk about you behind your back, and everyone listens.

Questions to Consider

- What promise do you make that you need to do a better job of keeping, every time, with every customer?
- In your company, who is responsible for your social media engagement with customers?
- Who is responsible for monitoring what customers are saying about you on the Internet?
- Do you actively seek out negative feedback from customers so that you know what they really think, or do you try to get only positive feedback?
- On a scale of 1 to 10, how would you rate your response to a dissatisfied customer?
- What is your process for engaging with unhappy customers?

19

Leadership

Grunder
Landscaping
Company

The Kid Was the Best

Marty Grunder started out mowing lawns when he was 13 years old. By the time he graduated from the University of Dayton in 1990, Grunder Landscaping Company had annual sales of $400,000 and six full-time employees. Let's just say that the kid was the best at what mattered most.

He still is. Marty's not a kid anymore, and he has taken Grunder Landscaping Company from his dad's tractor and a push mower that he bought at a garage sale to a reputation as one of the Midwest's most successful landscaping companies.

Marty is so respected in the green industry that in addition to running Grunder Landscaping, he teaches other landscapers all over the country how to take their companies to new levels of performance. He is a speaker, consultant, and coach, and he hosts field trips in which landscapers visit his company to learn about his leadership and management success. I've been speaking to business groups for more than 30 years, and I think that Marty is one of the most effective motivational speakers I've ever seen.

A few years ago Marty hired me to spend a day helping him with ideas on how to improve and grow his company. I don't know how impressed he was with me, but I came away from that day knowing that I had met one of the most effective leaders I'd ever worked with.

So what's the key to Marty's success? What's his philosophy about being the best at what matters the most? I talked with Marty about his approach to leadership, team building, and focus.

Joe: What matters most at Grunder Landscaping, Marty?
Marty: Everything starts with the vision, mission, and core values here. Our vision is where we aspire to be, what our

dream state is. The mission is what we are going to do on a daily basis to get to that dream state. The four core values are the behaviors we are going to embrace, eat, drink, and sleep here at GLC. You will not last here at Grunder if you don't embrace these values. And you will not pass the interview or be hired if we don't feel you are a fit for our core values. Our culture is what goes on when the boss isn't here. It's the very fiber that makes Grunder Landscaping better.

Joe: I know that Grunder Landscaping does a better job than most companies at making vision, mission, and values much more than words on a poster or a pocket card. It seems to be what guides everything that you do. Talk about that.

Marty: Our vision is to be recognized by our clients, our team members, and experts in our industry as the best landscaping company in our market area. Our mission is to enhance the beauty and value of every client's property while exceeding their expectations every step of the way. Our core values are quality, teamwork, leadership, and profitability. There's a lot that goes into those core values and every employee knows exactly what they mean.

The Responsibility of Leadership

Joe: What really impresses me, Marty, is that the people on your team go way beyond just memorizing all of this. I've seen countless examples of companies where the vision, mission, and values get dragged out for the quarterly employee meetings, but then go back in the drawer when the meeting's over. At Grunder, all of this is front and center all day long, every single day.

Marty: There are many ways small-business owners keep their teams focused, but this really gets to the responsibility of leadership. Steve Covey said it right when he said, "Begin with the end in mind." What is your desired state? What does a win look like? Too many business leaders miss this important first step. To get your team at your company to follow you, they have to have a reason to follow you. So your job then becomes to not only describe what the win looks like but also show each and every one of your people how their actions will contribute to or impede success.

Joe: So much of your leadership approach seems to be about pushing responsibility down and being able to delegate effectively.

Marty: In the process of growing my business from a truck and a push mower to what it is today, I have learned a lot. I have learned [that] to grow a business you have to learn how to delegate; otherwise, you won't grow. So if you want to grow, you have to entrust things to others. To entrust things to others, those people must not only understand what you need them to do but also have the personal motivation to do it. The "what's in it for me." If you can figure out how to get your team to do what you want and need them to do and have them feel great and passionate about that, you're on the right track.

Getting Buy-In

Joe: To get to that "what's in it for me" motivator, you have to get buy-in on what matters most from the team. I heard a CEO once say, "The decisions I make are useless unless I get buy-in from my 7,500 coworkers." What do you and your managers do to get buy-in?

Marty: At Grunder what matters most is a happy client. A lot goes into making a client happy. But we also know that our external customer service will never exceed our internal customer service. For our people to embrace our four core values, our leadership team has to show those behaviors ourselves, not just talk about them. If safety is important, a manager better work safely. If quality is important, a manager, a leader, can never say, "That's good enough." If communication is important, then as the owner, I'd better not make a habit of surprising people. In fact, surprises kill companies. They kill morale and stifle engagement. We have little red and white signs up all over the place that say "No Surprises." We take it very seriously here.

Joe: One of my core beliefs is that a leader should talk about what matters the most all the time. He or she should almost be a one-trick pony in constantly reinforcing what's important here. I've named you many times, Marty, as an example to other leaders in this regard.

Marty: Joe, for years as I was growing up as a person and a businessman, and this is all I've ever done, run Grunder Landscaping Company for 29 years, I thought that I was the only one who would believe in our vision or dream state of the company. At times, I would back off talking about our vision, mission, and core values, fearing that I was being a nag and not confident enough to be unwavering in my commitment to those things. I realized about 10 years ago that I had to stay on those things. I had to not only show by my actions that I believed in them but constantly be talking about them. I became not only the chief executive officer but also the chief reminding officer.

Spider-Man, Doughnuts, and Thank-You Notes

Joe: You do some things that most business owners or CEOs wouldn't do.

Marty: I've learned through the years ways to have fun with this, too. I dressed up like Spider-Man one time and taught my people to pay attention to the little things on a client's property, showing them to walk around a client property like Spider-Man, looking in every nook and cranny for the little things that a client would see that we did to show and to prove we really are better than our competition. We serve burgers to our employees once a month to serve them, since they are constantly serving us. I have an ice cream truck come in once in a while on a hot Friday to finish the day on a good note. I have stationed myself out in front of our office and stopped every truck that left to give out doughnuts and ask the crews what our vision, mission, and core values are. I've even had a local law enforcement officer stop our people at the end of our driveway to see if they have their seat belts on as safety is a huge part of our culture. And maybe most important, I have written hundreds of thank-you notes to members of our team, thanking them for specific things they have done well, sometimes including a photo of what they did, with the note. These are notes I mail to their homes, notes they can share with their family, notes that not only tell them I appreciate their support, but that I show them support in return. I have learned to spend a lot of time "catching people doing things right." That's been hard, as I am so wired for quality and excellence that I tend to be very critical. But I have also seen a person go on to the next level with a compliment.

A complaint usually doesn't have the same impact. The bottom line is that a positive, can-do leader tends to attract the same kind of people.

You Can't Just Put These Things on a Piece of Paper

Joe: It goes beyond having what matters most just be on a poster or a card.

Marty: The point is, you can't just put these things on a piece of paper and expect everyone to not only to understand them but to live them. I tell my team not only do they need to know what our mission statement is and understand it, but more important, they need to work like they are on a mission.

Joe, I know that you always say, "Culture drives results"—that is so very true. I am proud of our culture, but it took a long time to get here. It takes a lot of talking, and a lot of doing, constantly reminding everyone what we are trying to do. And recognizing those employees who are supporting our culture and sending those who aren't on down the road.

Talk about It and Live It All the Time

Joe: You said once that if you're really effective as a leader, your people will make fun of you.

Marty: This is one of the truest things I can share with you from my experience as an entrepreneur. When you get the right people on your team, and you're really getting through to them, you'll know it, because you will catch them mocking you stating your vision, mission, and core value statements, because you talk about it and live it all the time. But more important, you'll be able to brag about what you are capable of doing with clients and prospects because of the results you have been getting.

He Is True North

I think at the core of what makes Marty Grunder a successful businessman and leader is his character. He runs deep. The guy has absolute clarity on what matters most, and as Kris Kristofferson once said about Johnny Cash, "He is true North." Marty Grunder is the real deal, and to see how he walks the talk with his team every single day is to take a master's course in leadership.

Questions to Consider

- If someone chose one of your employees at random and asked, "What's really important here?," what would he or she say?
- Does everyone know what's important here? How do you know?
- What do you do to continually reinforce what matters most in your organization?
- Do you constantly remind everyone or yourself what matters most?
- If someone chose one of your customers at random and asked, "What matters most?" in regard to your business, what would he or she say?
- What are the three things you do, either as a leader of others or alone, that you believe are most effective in

creating positive, constructive motivation for excellent performance? (It's fine to say, "You can't motivate others. They have to do it for themselves." But as a leader, it's a total cop-out to think that it's not your responsibility to create an environment that is supportive of positive motivation.)

- Are your employees happy?
- If not, how is it working out to have unhappy employees dealing with one another and with customers?

20

When Everything Is Pursued, the Important Is Neglected

Too Much Pressure

Sometimes, to get to the really important things in our work or our lives, we have to let go. We have to create the space for what matters most to take its place.

I have a seven-year-old daughter, and like her big sister before her, she loves the Berenstain Bears series of children's books. One book in the series has some very real applications to anyone who is chasing every imaginable idea and tactic they see to try to improve their business.

The book is *The Berenstain Bears and Too Much Pressure*. It's a classic tale of a family whose schedule gets out of control. Much like the business owner or manager who is spread too thin and unable to get the team focused on what matters most, the Berenstain Bears have created a pressure-cooker life in which, because everything is pursued, the most important things are neglected.

Sister Bear's Nightmare

In the story, Sister Bear has a nightmare. "Sister dreamed she was on a strange sort of merry-go-round . . . a merry-go-round of activities which went round and round and round. She wanted to get off, but no matter how hard she tried, she couldn't."

I've had business owners and managers tell me they are experiencing much the same kind of nightmare in real life. "We're working like mad. Nobody goes home before 10:00 PM around here," they say, "but it seems like we can never do enough to get us where we need to be."

Executing in the Game They Are In

My friend Randy Pennington, a leading expert on creating cultures that drive results, says, "Most leaders look for the game changer when what they really need to do is get better at executing in the game they are in." For me, boiling that thought down to its essence means that I should stop looking for more things to do. Sometimes I need to just get better at what I'm already doing. That doesn't mean being stagnant. On the contrary, constant improvement means constant change and innovation.

Purpose versus Panic

It's fascinating to me that successful companies always seem to be in a state of constant, purposeful, focused change. The change is looked upon as necessary and, more significantly, normal. Even though the changes may be intense, no one is upset.

Companies that are struggling, by contrast, approach change in a state of frenzied upset and what can even look like panic. Mediocre companies change when something's wrong. Successful companies change so that things won't go wrong in the first place.

Change and constant improvement don't have to be like the Berenstain Bears' merry-go-round of stress and pressure. You can approach change in a reasoned, planned, methodical way and be infinitely more effective and innovative as a result.

For many years I've talked about the power of letting go of what's getting in the way of your own success. The idea certainly isn't original to me. Warren Buffett said, "The difference between successful people and very successful people is that very successful people say 'no' to almost every-thing." Your what-to-stop-doing list may, in fact, have much more potential positive power for you than your to-do list.

Take a look at the following list. There may be things on this list that you believe have meaning for you. Even if you believe that nothing on the list relates to you, use it as a way to start thinking about what you need to stop doing or let go of.

What Do You Need to STOP Doing?

STOP waiting for someone else to "fix it."

STOP worrying about things that you have no control over.

STOP sending 25 e-mails when it could be resolved with a 5-minute phone call.

STOP trying to make something work that's never going to.

STOP avoiding people whom you need to meet with.

STOP trying to do everything perfectly and just do it.

STOP listening to gossip or wasting time with negative people. You need to do more to help people in other areas of the company. You need to ask for help when you need it. You need to be more self-reliant and get it done yourself. You need to focus on what's most important and stop wasting time on the unimportant.

STOP doing it the way you do it because it's the way you've always done it. You need to invest more in yourself and your professional development. You need to focus on the basics.

STOP having to be right and making the other guy wrong. You need to spend more face-to-face time with people.

STOP spending too much time with people and not enough at your desk.

STOP trying to do everything yourself.

STOP tolerating inconsistent performance.

STOP hoping that the person causing the problem will somehow miraculously change. You need to take action.

STOP putting off the decision that you know you must make immediately.

STOP procrastinating and start implementing.

STOP dwelling on what's wrong. Start making it right.

21

The Rules You Can Break

"Fortunately, We Don't Know Any of Them"

Which rules can you break? All of them.

Except possibly one, which is the rule that you have to, at some point, make a profit. Even in a nonprofit organization you still obviously have to make the numbers work. So that's the one rule you can't break. As for the rest of them, keep the ones that work for you and break the rest. Make up new ones. Your goal shouldn't be to run your business the way experts say you have to. Your goal should be to run your business in the way that works best.

> There are three rules for running a business; fortunately, we don't know any of them.
>
> —*Paul Newman, Newman's Own*

Visions and Missions Are Great—and Optional

But doesn't every business have to have vision and mission statements? Lots of them do, and it works well for them. But if it doesn't work for you, you can replace your vision and mission statements with, for example, a simple list of what matters most to you if that is more effective. You can go with one sentence or one word or three words. There are some who will read this and think it's a misprint. "Did he just say that we don't have to have a vision statement? Or a mission statement? Oh my word! What kind of crazy talk is that?"

I know companies that thrive, grow, and make money hand over fist and have never written the first word of a vision or mission statement. Vision and mission statements are perfectly good ways to organize your thoughts around what matters most, but you don't have to do it that way. Seriously. In the 30 years that I've worked with every kind of business imaginable, I've seen more useless vision statements than I can remember.

I remember one vision statement for an emergency care center company. It was a classic corporate-speak statement about serving communities and being the leader in delivering high-quality health care and everything else that a Vision Statement 101 class in a business school would teach you to include. It meant nothing to anyone there. In a company leadership meeting I finally got one of the senior management team to tell me, in her own words, what she thought her company was all about. "We help people when they're hurt."

I did a quick survey of the room and found that there was an almost unanimous agreement that those words meant more and were more motivating to them than the vision statement. Ditto for the mission statement. I offered them a radical suggestion, "So why don't you just use those words? Why don't you replace your vision and mission statements with 'We help people when they're hurt'?"

You can do that, you know. Or you can stick with or develop your vision and mission statements to your heart's content. Please let go of doing things the way other people tell you they should be done. It's your business, and it doesn't necessarily fit some preconceived model that someone else says you should follow.

One Size Does Not Fit All

Some companies absolutely thrive with the vision, mission, and values model. Grunder Landscaping Company, featured earlier in this book, is a prime example of creating, sustaining, and growing a business with total team focus on vision, mission, and values. For many, it's not only a logical way to approach the business, but one that serves to motivate and even inspire top performance.

Another company in this book, Smile Brands, has clarity on what matters most through a simple statement of "Deliver Smiles for Everyone." Leaders there say that "whether you call it our vision, mission, or purpose, it is the reason for Smile Brands' existence and what each employee and affiliated dental provider strives for every day." The leaders at Smile Brands aren't hung up on how you label it. They just know that it's what's most important.

The point is that one size does not fit all. There are other approaches to creating focus and purpose that could work better for you. One of my favorite examples of a non-traditional approach is discussed in Chapter 5. It's the advertising agency that I read about that began with four things that were most important to the three owners:

1. Do great work.
2. Have fun.
3. Make money.
4. Don't work with people you can't stand.

I love this. Absolutely love it. It might be the worst approach in the world for you, but I love that these three owners decided that they'd forego the vision, mission, and values approach and simply make a list of the four things that mattered most to them.

Changing the World . . . Maybe

Note something else about the advertising agency's list. It doesn't include anything that most people would consider particularly inspiring, although I have to admit that it inspires me a lot more than the typical, tedious vision or mission statement. There's no higher purpose or lofty goal. I don't see a word about changing the world or making people's lives better. Without a really meaningful vision that gives them something bigger than themselves to work for, can they succeed?

Of course they can. In past few years I'd be really challenged to find a book about business or a motivational speaker who didn't say something about the requirement that you and all of your employees simply must have a higher cause to work for or your business won't succeed.

That's silly. Really. There's one Fortune 500 company that many business speakers and writers say is successful because everyone there wants to "change the world." Just for fun, I asked employees in three of that company's retail stores in three different cities, "Why do you work here?" (I was researching the company for another book that I wrote.)

Their answers ranged from "Because I just love working on this stuff" to "This is a very cool company, and they let us do what we're good at," from "This mall is about 2 minutes from my house, and I can ride my bike to work" to "The people I work with are more fun than anywhere else I've ever worked." Not one mention of changing the world. Not one.

It's a great company, and I'm sure that in company headquarters there are probably some people who go to work every day motivated and driven by the idea of changing the world. That is a good and noble thing, and if it motivates them to do great work, then it is absolutely effective as their definition for what matters most. But that aspiration doesn't necessarily flow through the hearts and minds of everyone else in the company. It might even be a barrier to top performance for some because it's simply not what motivates them.

Everywhere I see inspiring, cool, creative stories about companies and people in business that sound wonderful and lead us to great thoughts about how world-changing our businesses can be. But back in the real world there are employees who may not be inspired or motivated by the same things that get the senior leadership team all excited. One thing I love about Charles and Julie May at bytes of knowledge (see Chapter 14) is their understanding of what motivates their employees and their willingness to incorporate those motivations into the company agenda to accomplish the goals for the company.

"We Make Great Carburetors"

The concept of what matters most has got to be very personal to you and your people. This statement of focus and purpose should reach people on an emotional level, which could mean "We save the world" or could mean "We make great carburetors." Don't get hung up on thinking that you have to include "We also want to be healthy, protect the environment, and contribute to the well-being of the world"—unless, of course, it really rings true.

A Purpose That Took Morale Lower

Many years ago, a big bank I worked with decided to roll out a new internal statement of purpose—and it actually drove morale lower. It said "XYZ Bank, where every employee matters and makes a difference." When they unveiled that statement to the troops, you could almost hear the eyes rolling out of people's heads and careening down the hallways. "Really?" the employees were saying behind the backs of the leaders. "I mean, *really?*" The feeling was pretty unanimous among the employees that none of them mattered to the company and that nobody made a difference. The company actually lost ground and took morale lower than ever with their ridiculous attempt at motivation. Some things are so dumb that it's hard to even respond to it. That's how dumb this was.

You're Kidding, Right?

Sometimes we fall into the trap of saying things that we think we should because the Vision Statement 101 Handbook says we should. I often stop by a local grocery store that is part of a big regional chain. They used to have their vision statement on a big sign hanging in the store right in front of the checkout lines.

I was reading that vision statement one day when it struck me how silly it was. It said, in part, "We are the most innovative neighborhood store in the country." What? Are you serious? You're kidding, right?

This is a good grocery store with a great selection and competitive prices. That's its strength. But innovative? I didn't see it. Add to that the fact that it was within three blocks of two truly innovative grocery stores, Trader Joe's and Whole Foods. Further consider that its vision statement wasn't even limited to being the most innovative grocery store but stated that it was the most innovative neighborhood store, period.

The store was located across the street from an Apple retail store. And it thinks it's the most innovative neighborhood store in America? Sorry.

So what's the point of a vision statement like that? Why claim that you are the best at something that's not even one of your strengths. It makes me think that somebody went to a three-day leadership "visioning" retreat with some consultant who suggested innovation as a worthy goal, and the group looks at each other, nods heads, and says, "Sure. Innovation. That sounds good. Put it on the flip chart."

It's Just Supposed to Be Effective

How you determine what matters most and the way you make that work for you and your business aren't supposed to be anything except one thing: effective. My hope is that, if nothing else, this book will give you permission to let go of any "rules" that you think you have to follow even if you know they aren't a good fit for you.

I'm not talking about the rules of good business practices or ethics or the reality of making the numbers work. Of course we have to be responsible in our conduct of business. But don't feel tied to visions or missions or anything else that doesn't fit who you are and how you work most effectively.

Remember, being the best at what matters most means what matters most to you, your team, and your customers. It's not about what matters most to any other company and certainly not what matters most to me or any other business "expert."

You are the expert. Do it your way.

Questions to Consider

- Look at whatever statement you presently have of what matters most. Whether it is a vision statement, a mission statement, values, or so on, look at it or all of them and answer this question: On a scale of 1 to 10,

how effective is your_____?
(vision statement, mission statement, etc.)

- What do you need to do to make it more effective?
- Do you need to completely rethink your approach?
- Should you change the wording of it?
- Should you simply tweak it?
- Should you leave it as is?
- Do you need to throw it all out and start over?
- Would changing it reenergize your organization or just prove distracting?
- Who should participate in this process?
- Does your statement of what matters most reach people on an emotional level?
- If not, does that matter to you?
- Is your statement of what matters most written from your hearts and minds, or is it written according to how you think it is supposed to sound?

22

Focus 3
Ninety

What Matters Most Right Now?

It's easy to get stuck in the trap of overthinking things. That trap becomes especially dangerous (and tempting) when we're thinking about "big" questions like what matters most. I've been on those two- and three-day strategic planning retreats where everyone sat around a U-shaped configuration of tables and used up dozens of pages of flip chart paper as they attempted to come up with the big answers to the big questions such as "What are our highest, greatest aspirations?" or "How can we make a difference in the world?" or "What do we offer that is completely unique and can't be done by anyone else?"

Quite honestly, after participating in more of those kinds of visioning sessions than I can count, I have to say that most of them produce less-than-optimal results. The pressures of time and just wanting to get something down on paper so that we can say we succeeded often end up resulting in grand statements that just don't ring true on a gut level.

I'll say it again: No one is a bigger fan of doing grand and glorious things than I am. I vote yes. I also vote yes on sometimes just saying, "Let's make great carburetors," and getting on with it. Consider that you might be best serviced by whittling things down to size for now so that you can take action and start creating better results. Let's shift the question from what matters most in our universe to what matters most right now for our company and our customers.

One of the great benefits of taking an intentional and focused approach to what we need to improve right now is that the process can begin to reveal what matters most in a big-picture way. Taking action always produces new information and insights, and doing something is usually more productive than just thinking about doing something.

A New Approach to Focus?

As I discussed earlier, many companies experience great success using the traditional model of vision, mission, and strategy. That's great, and if it works for you, I encourage you to continue defining what matters most using that model. For others, however, a new approach can prove to be more productive.

The traditional way that many companies determine where their focus should be is through, first, a vision statement. A vision statement can be described as a statement of purpose in terms of guiding values. Many business writers and consultants say that it's where you should state your higher purpose that will provide the motivation for everyone in the organization.

The mission statement also defines purpose but usually more in terms of objectives and measurements. In simplest terms, the vision statement defines where we're going and the mission statement defines what we do to get there. But let's not get caught up in the semantics of what a vision or mission statement should look like. Let's consider a different or additional approach to how we establish our focus.

Where Do We Improve Right Now?

It can get easy for the beautifully crafted vision and mission statements to fade into the wallpaper and become those dusty documents that get dragged down at each employee meeting, only to be put back up on the wall after the meeting is over. Far too often they are so lofty and idealistic that they serve no earthly purpose and do no practical good. You might do well to consider trying a new or additional way of creating focus and driving action.

I've had success working with companies on a short-term approach to creating permanent improvements in performance. The program is called Focus 3 Ninety. Like so many of the ideas in this book, it is powerful in part because it is so simple. Try this approach: What three things do we need to improve in the next 90 days?

It should take you and the right people in your organization no more than half a day to come up with the three things that you should improve, all related to what matters most to your business. One great advantage of this short-term approach is that no one feels locked in or that any permanent decisions are being made. Just three things to improve in 90 days.

Make It Last

Don't waste time on quick-fix improvements that simply entail a temporary rush of activity. Think in terms of improvements you can make in processes over the next 90 days. For example, don't have the sales force do 90 days of temporarily making more sales calls. Instead, look at your selling process for places where you can make permanent improvements. Improve the way you research prospects and prepare for calls so that you permanently improve your conversion rate going forward.

Get Absolute Clarity

The key to making this work will be to have absolute clarity in terms of:

- The specific improvements you want to make
- How you will measure your success

- Who is accountable for each of the three areas of improvement
- The support that each of those people is given
- The schedule and checkpoints along the way

It simply does not have to be more complicated than that.

This exercise isn't about painstakingly wordsmithing any statements of any kind. You just sit down and make a list of three things to improve in 90 days. By the way, it doesn't have to be three things. It can be two or four, or possibly five. The point is to create focus.

What You'll Learn

When I work with groups on this process, it's amazing how effective people can be when you give them a simple challenge like this and say, "Figure it out." They almost always do. When they get balled up in disagreements or begin arguing about finding three simple things to improve, that's valuable too, because it indicates that there are some serious disconnects that need to be addressed.

As you go through the process of identifying and implementing the improvements, you may glean valuable insight into what truly does matter most to you and your customers. At the end of the 90 days, do an assessment of what's been accomplished, then move forward with a new set of three things to improve, or keep the ones in place that you feel need more focus and attention.

You might find that this short-term focus is more effective for you and your team than following objectives as set out in a mission statement. And there's no need to worry about losing your way or drifting off course as long as you have a clear set of values as your foundation. It's always your values and culture that create stability through times of change, and these days we are always in a time of change.

Questions to Consider

- What specific improvements do you want to make?
- How will you measure our success?
- Who is accountable for each of the three areas of improvement?
- What support or resources will each of those people need?
- What are the schedule and checkpoints along the way?

23
It's 11:30

Taking Action

My clients often ask, "How can we be better at taking action?" I tell them to decide what's important, then do it. Of course, no one ever buys this as a sufficient answer, so there's always the follow-up question, "But how?"

To understand how an organization takes action, I go back to something my friend and sometimes consulting partner, Chuck Feltz, had to say. Feltz, aside from being an extraordinary consultant and business advisor, has been a C-level leader in a number of companies. A few years ago, when he was the president of a 20,000-employee company, I asked him how he was able to be so effective at getting his team to get things done.

He gave me a somewhat perplexed look, as if it were an odd question, and said, "We get clarity on what we need to do, and I assign someone to do it. I make them accountable, we come up with a schedule, and I give them the resources they need. They report back to me at an agreed-upon time on their progress. If there are problems or obstacles, we solve those and move forward until completion. How else would you do it?"

So, for those of you wondering how you get people in an organization to take action, let's review: clarity on what needs to be done, accountability, scheduling, problem solving, and done. Questions? Okay. Let's move on.

The Obstacle of Not Knowing

What about the individual who just can't seem to get going and take action on what matters most?

The biggest obstacle to action for a lot of people is not knowing what matters most. We've been going over that idea throughout the book, so now we should be at the point where you need to actually do something.

In my case, what matters most in terms of activity is doing quality work on, for example, this book. Ultimately, you will be the one who decides whether it's a good and useful book, but what I know is that I have to go to my office, turn on my computer, and start writing. Periodically, I review what I've written and often end up throwing it out. I then write more. I do that all day or until I feel like my brain is too mushy to do quality creative work. Then I do something else that matters most, like work on an upcoming program for a client, make calls, or send e-mails in the interest of being a pleasure and easy for my clients, partners, and colleagues to work with. I do things like respond quickly with whatever information they requested or ship the books they ordered so that they arrive early or thank them for something they did that I appreciate.

Then I get to things like making bank deposits, going through the mail, and so on. Some people work most effectively by doing all the administrative stuff before they get to what matters most. That's fine. Find your rhythm and go with it. Work the way you work best.

Take Out the Trash

So that's how it works. But some people will still say, "But how? How can I get better at taking action?"

Do you have to take the trash out at home? If so, how do you do that? I mean, how do you make that happen? What if you just aren't good at taking action?

Here's how it works. It's time for bed. You know that one of the things that matters most in keeping your home in order is to take out the trash. So you get up, turn off the television, walk into the kitchen, and take the full trash bag out of its container. You take it outside and put it in the garbage can.

And that's how you do it.

Someone Busier Than You Is Running

So do that at work. If you need inspiration, go find a Nike ad that says, "Just do it," and hang it in front of your desk. Or better yet, find the Nike poster I saw in a store window that said, "Somewhere someone busier than you is running right now." Or imagine the reward or payoff you'll get for taking action. Or simply wait until the pain of not taking action is greater than the perceived pain of taking action. Or get someone to be your action buddy and hold each other accountable. Or hire a coach. I did that a few years ago. We'd talk once a week by phone, and she was terrific at holding my feet to the fire on things that I'd decided mattered the most. She was just relentless in making me do what I knew I needed to do.

Look, one way or another we're either going to do the things we know we need to do or we're not. Seriously, how do we answer that question, "How can I take action?" That thing you say you want to do is either a priority to you or it's not.

It's 11:30

On Sunday afternoon my 10-year-old daughter, Jessica, asked me if she and her best friend, Emma, could set up a lemonade stand in our yard. It was a very drizzly, wet, cool day. But I thought a lesson could be learned about disappointment and realistic expectations, so I said, "Sure." They painted a sign ("50 Cents a Cup—All Proceeds to Benefit Animal Shelter"), made the lemonade, set up their table in the yard, and stood in the drizzle. I sighed the sigh that a wise parent sighs as his child is about to face disappointment.

Finally, a lone, soggy jogger stopped. Then a car. Then neighbors started coming over. *Then* the Grey Line tour bus comes to a screeching halt right in front of our house. (I'm in Nashville. Two country music stars live in my neighborhood. Not unusual.) The tour bus driver opened his door, ordered a cup of lemonade, then invited the girls to bring their pitcher onto the bus and almost every passenger bought a cup. After two hours, the girls had made almost $60 for the animal shelter.

A valuable lesson was learned—not by them, by me. The lesson was that sometimes, even when everything seems stacked against you, you just go. It's just your time.

As Andy Samberg of *Saturday Night Live* once said, "We don't start the show because we're ready. We start the show because it's 11:30."

For Jess and Emma, it was 11:30.

Look at your watch.

Questions to Consider

- What time is it? Is it time to go?
- If not now, when?
- How long can you afford to wait?
- Is your competition waiting?
- How long will your customers let us wait?

24

Ideas That Matter Most

- Get your thinking clean enough to make things simple.
- We don't get hurt by what we don't know. We get hurt by what we know and don't do.
- Be so good at the basics that you're cutting edge.
- Be the best at what matters most, and you will succeed.
- The winners aren't the ones who do the most things. The winners are the ones who do the most important things.
- "Pressure is what you feel when you don't know what the hell you're doing." —Peyton Manning
- You are using a flamethrower when you should be using a blue-tip flame from an acetylene torch. (Concept from Peter Sheahan.)
- There aren't any silver bullets. Not one. There's quality. That's not a bullet. It's the bomb. It always wins.
- Make a better car. Make a better hamburger.
- The important thing is to find out what's the most important thing and get to work on it.
- "Step away from your computer and go find some real live customers." —Dr. Jeff Cornwall
- "If it's worth doing, it's worth doing wrong." —Arnie Malham
- Being the best is a moving target. You have to constantly improve and innovate.
- "We do not especially like meetings but recognize the absolute necessity to keep everyone on the same page and fully informed." —Chris Clothier
- "Simplicity is the ultimate sophistication." —Leonardo da Vinci
- "Bells and whistles wear off, but usefulness never does." —37signals
- Simplicity and focus are your force multipliers.
- More isn't better. Better is better.
- "Plug the holes in the bucket." —Julie May

- Culture drives results.
- "Surprises kill companies." —Marty Grunder
- "There are three rules for running a business; fortunately, we don't know any of them." —Paul Newman
- "We don't start the show because we're ready. We start the show because it's 11:30." —Andy Samberg

25

More Resources

There truly are no secrets of success. Everything you need to know about how to make your business more successful is already out there. I've listed just a handful of resources that I find valuable and that I recommend to you.

Elizabeth Crook of Orchard Advisors is a genius at helping companies get focused. Orchard Advisors is at orchard advisors.com. Elizabeth's new book is *The Yippee Index: Live The Life YOU Love At Work*

Risky Is the New Safe, by Randy Gage

The Outstanding Organization: Generate Business Results by Eliminating Chaos and Building the Foundation for Everyday Excellence, by Karen Martin

The Checklist Manifesto: How to Get Things Right, by Atul Gawande

Making It Happen: Turning Good Ideas into Great Results, by Peter Sheahan

Michael Heard is a principal of 3 Big Questions, a consultancy that "helps organizations triage, stabilize, and prioritize action plans through facilitation and conflict resolution services." Michael can be reached at michael@3bigques tions.com.

Marty Grunder's not only a great business leader but also a great speaker. You can reach Marty at MartyGrunder .com.

Index

Calloway/*Becoming a Category of One*
ISBN 978-0-470-49635-0

Becoming a Category of One reveals how extraordinary companies do what they do so well and gives you the tools and ideas to help your business emulate their success. Packed with real case studies and personal reflections from successful business leaders, it helps you apply the best practices of the best companies to set yourself apart from your competitors and turn your business into a market leader.

Calloway/*Work Like You're Showing Off!*
ISBN 978-0-470-11626-5

Showing off is a good thing. Showing off is a mind-set. Showing off is about living life and doing work in a way that creates joy, jazz, and a kick in our lives and in the lives of those around us. This is a business book for almost everyone—from executives and managers to receptionists and sales clerks. Here's the key: Success is an inside job. After 26 years of studying and working with top performers, Joe Calloway shares the key factors in creating success, without pulling any punches. *Work Like You're Showing Off!* isn't for sissies; it's a tough, realistic approach to getting the most out of life by giving more to others.

Calloway/*Indispensable*
ISBN 978-0-471-70308-2

When products and services become interchangeable, price becomes the ultimate determinant for consumers. *Indispensable* shows businesses how to break out of that cycle by using The Five Drivers, a strategy that takes companies to the next level of performance. Renowned business consultant Joe Calloway looks at how real companies have made their product or service "mission critical" and satisfied customers in the process.